## Praise For *Priestess*

"Julie's book is so important for now. Julie is a modern-day priestess, a dear Sister of the 'Clan of Encouragement' and a welcome role model for feminine leadership. Julie 'walks her talk'. Her book serves as an informative educational work to enable the necessary reclaiming of women's spirituality. It is both a calling and a call to action. Julie weaves her personal story, with the stories of priestesses from many different cultures and a 'how to guide' to connect with one's priestess self/nature. She offers suggestions for practices including reconnection to the cycles—seasons, moon and menstrual cycle—which form a guide for the necessary inner work required by us all to be, as a lineage holder of the School of Shamanic Womancraft would say - the Women the Earth needs now. I hope everyone recognises themselves through Julie's encouraging offering and reclaims themselves through one of the many different ways to priestess that she presents."

— **Jane Hardwicke Collings**, midwife, teacher of the Women's Mysteries and founder of The School of Shamanic Womancraft


"What a gift Julie Parker has given us with her divine book, *Priestess*. It is a rare book filled with ancient wisdom and modern teachings, that is so needed in the world today. A guidebook for spiritual leaders and those wishing to evolve into one, *Priestess* teaches us to not only find the sacred path for ourselves, but to light that path in an inclusive way for everyone, as our sacred duty. This book is essential reading for everyone who identifies with the path of the priestess, with the Goddess, with new paths of leadership and activism, with a life of sacred spiritual practice. May *Priestess* reach the hearts and souls of everyone who needs Her magic."

—**Megan Dalla-Camina**, author of *Simple Soulful Sacred: A Woman's Guide to Clarity, Comfort and Coming Home to Herself* (Hay House)


"In this extraordinary chronicling of the priestesses of then, now and always, Julie Parker says there is no road map. And yet ... this book guides us straight into the centre of it all. All that is, all that there was and all that is to come. With strong hand, supple heart and all-seeing eyes, she takes us beyond the over-trodden land of "love and light" into the dark and cool labyrinthian land of power, sisterhood, justice, reverence. This book is a reclamation and a reckoning. With grit and grace and humour and beauty and poetry and righteous anger and loving kindness, Julie takes us there. 'I am here. And ready to be counted'."

—**Tanya Geisler**, leadership coach

"I have not been genuinely excited by a book in the spiritual genre until Julie's book came my way. I have been a solitary priestess for a decade, and it was Julie's work that brought me to commune with other priestesses. I am forever grateful. The priestess in me did heart leaps as I dove into the pages of *Priestess*. This is a must-read book for every womxn alive today. Julie has woven every part of herself through these pages and brought topics to the table that cannot be overlooked in priestess awakening. *Priestess* brought forth tears, joy, strength, boldness, compassion and most of all, so much love. Julie embodies *Priestess* in all that she does and this book is one which will leave a meaningful legacy for every generation of womxn to come."

—**Sharyn Holmes,** founder of Gutsy Girl and Formidable Voices

"*Priestess* is so much more than a guide. It's an inner igniting, it's an activation. It's an invitation to meet and connect with your true priestess self that has always lived within you. It's a calling up - into your truth, your deep knowing, your feminine power. It's a journey of coming home. *Priestess* is a potent and important companion for the modern spiritual leader who is ready to deepen into all that is divine within her and around her. It's rich in reverence, insights and is a deep remembering of our truth as spiritual leaders, bursting with ancient teachings presented in a modern and grounded way for the spiritual leaders of our times. This is a book you'll keep coming back to and one to gift every woman you know who's on her spiritual path."

—**Sammie Fleming,** life coach and sacred circle facilitator

"Women around the world are feeling a pull to be of greater service as Mother Earth awakens the dormant part of ourselves that lifetimes ago was deeply connected to her rhythms. The memories of being a healer, ceremonialist, warrior, wayshower, and so much more come to us like a vague dream and disrupts the way we have lived life. A powerful handmaiden who has already removed her veil has arrived to help ground us to our history, help us claim ourselves in this present time while encouraging us to change our future. This is the sovereign *Priestess*, Julie Parker. I cannot express my deepest gratitude for Julie and the sacred book *Priestess*. This object that you have in your hand is more than words written on paper. This is a palimpsest where underneath the words is a sacred manuscript that has energetically been weaved in to help you remember who you are. Allow *Priestess* to help you track the history of others that have come before you. Allow *Priestess* to be the portal into your temple space where you become the Modern Priestess owning your medicine and mastering your craft. The time is now."

— **Sora Surya No**, business coach, co-founder of priestess temple school, sacred business collective and host of Sora TV

"*Priestess* is the transformational book you didn't know you needed – until now! With *Priestess*, you receive the trifecta of a dear sister, motivational speaker and performance coach all alchemised into one. It's like she's right there sitting next to you in circle, or coaching you as her client, or standing on a large stage being of service to her audience. Reading Julie's words feels like she is in conversation with just you, supporting you in practical and beautiful ways as you go about navigating modern life. I can see my future self, reaching into my bookshelf for *Priestess* whenever I need guidance, clarity, or a loving (and fairly firm!) nudge to just hurry up and take action already! Julie's words are delightfully personable, encouragingly practical and of course, all gorgeously curated to make this the go-to book for all modern-day priestesses."

—**Michaela Rosandich,** cycle superpowers coach at Empress Crow and Rabbit

"Finally! A loving reference book, personal priestess journey activator, call to action for humankind and irresistible invitation to live beyond fear combined, *Priestess: Ancient Spiritual Wisdom for Modern Sacred Women* is without doubt the modern-day companion for all heart-centered leaders and connection seekers. With unparalleled clarity and accessibility, Julie Parker has held open the door to a more powerful way of being, reflecting, living and serving while honouring deep remembrance and the individuality of the woman and priestess within. It is crucial reading and I will be thumbing its pages again and again."

—**Johanna Parker,** founder of Heart Sparks

"I came to know myself as I never had before.
If these words cause a stirring in your soul, then Julie Parker's *Priestess: Ancient Spiritual Wisdom for Modern Sacred Women* will delight and uplift you. Not only will you learn all about priestesses past and present, but a desire will likely be awakened within to deepen the journey along your spiritual path towards a place of sovereignty, integrity and personal power. This is a wonderful book to challenge, inform and lovingly hold space for you to ignite your inner priestess."

—**Melissa Jeffcott,** certified life coach and sacred space holder

"Never have I read a book that makes me feel so validated, seen and understood as a modern-day priestess. Julie Parker's *Priestess* is not only a practical guide, it's also a balm for the soul. On every page, she has taken care to acknowledge the complexity of the priestess path, from the shadow and the light, the love and the rage, the service and the stillness. Much more than crystals and flower crowns, being a priestess is about radical self-acceptance, wild liberation, and a daily commitment to a calling that comes from deep within. I will treasure this book and its invaluable wisdom for years to come."

—**Jolinda Johnson,** women's health coach

"Where do I begin? *Priestess* is a must-read for all women! I love, love, loved it. It's one of those books that I know I will come back to time and time again. Julie Parker has a unique gift of making you feel truly seen, heard and loved in her presence, and that's exactly how it feels reading this book. *Priestess* is more than a book, it's a call to action. To reclaim and embrace all parts of ourselves. To be of service, to speak up and take action for the betterment of ourselves and others. To explore our innate gifts and talents. To commune and create a deeper connection with Mama Earth, Goddess and most importantly ourselves. To witness our greatness and sovereignty within. To remember our divine purpose in this lifetime is to simply be our whole, true selves. What a gift. Thank you, Julie, for writing this book and so much more."

—**Jade Head,** priestess and holistic health and life coach

"Julie's *Priestess* is a gentle initiation into a world of sovereignty, homecoming, leadership, sacred living and inner wisdom. Julie effortlessly weaves together the modern and the ancient, the practical and the magical, bringing us closer to who we really are and illuminating what the word priestess might mean to each of us. Julie offers practices and mythology coupled with her own story, as a springboard to create or continue to evolve our own understandings of what it means to be a modern sacred leader.
Julie dives far beyond an exploration of spirituality that revolves around flower crowns, crystals and Instagram-worthy circles. From the ongoing impacts of patriarchal culture, reclaiming our power as cyclic beings, working with the goddess, abandoning the notion of perfection, people-pleasing and judgment, living with fear, embracing the dark and calling out racism and exclusion in our own spiritual communities. What emerges is the overarching sense that we are not alone on this journey and that a vital part of the priestess journey is an acknowledgement and active commitment to dismantling the external structural forces that serve to oppress, harm and maintain inequalities that cannot be loved and lighted away."

—**Bronwyn Stange,** founder of Bopo Women

"*Priestess* is a coming home, an embodiment, a deep remembering of sovereign feminine within. Julie's words, deep study and inclusive understanding of the priestess invites us all to look both inward *and towards one another* to see the strong, wild, fierce, gentle, feminine leader wanting to emerge. The words and spirit of *Priestess* will evoke you to remember, embody, celebrate and be in service of the Great Mother – her spirit and soul that resides within each of us. Thank you, Julie, for saying YES to bringing the sacred work of *Priestess* to the world. We needed her. I needed her."

—**Madison Morrigan,** life coach

"I devoured Julie's *Priestess* book, soaking in all the ancient wisdom gathered together with such reverence. These pages are glorious, brimming with sacred feminine GOLD! Thank you, Julie, this is truly magnificent."

—**Loren Honey,** intuitive life coach, sacred circle facilitator and energy worker

"Spirituality with substance! Rich in research this book is sure to resonate with those lucky enough to be drawn to all things Priestess."

— **Emma Mildon,** bestselling author of *The Soul Searcher's Handbook* and *Evolution of Goddess*

"Traversing ancient priestess her-stories, weaving in everyday rituals and modern-day archetypes, and culminating with the powerful call to "strap on your boots!" to make a purposeful contribution with your gifts, this is THE sacred leadership guidebook for the modern priestess!"

—**Dr. Ezzie Spencer,** bestselling author of the book and journal *Lunar Abundance*, and creator of re.love

"A deep dive into the world of the *Priestess*. Julie's empowering way of weaving words into such an expansive read of all things priestess and the Goddess will infuse your whole being with a richness of simply 'knowing', a stepping back into a deeper sense of self as She will awaken something from within. The personal knowledge shared, researched history of and the modern-day actions you are guided to journey with through *Priestess* will expand your heart, mind, body and soul in ways you've never explored before. The pages of *Priestess* will captivate you from the moment you open the book, and Julie's delicious storytelling will hold you in a loving embrace the whole way through – you can literally hear Her speak it to you – and you'll find it hard NOT to put down. *Priestess* is an honouring of the sacred that lies within us all. I bow down in such deep gratitude, again, to Julie's devotion in keeping the wisdom of the priestess alive on Mother Earth."

—**Tracey Pattison**, priestess to Mother Earth, intuitive food consultant, coach for womxn and recipe creatrix for bestselling cookbooks

"*Priestess* is both a remembrance and a revelation. Julie's wisdom serves as a potent invitation to women everywhere to turn their gaze inward, activate their innate feminine power, and fully live the truth of who they are.
In honouring the vast lineage of sacred leaders that came before, *Priestess* will guide you home to the understanding of what it truly means to live and lead from your soul, as a modern-day priestess.
This is a divine book you won't want to put down, and a must-have companion for your spiritual journey."

—**Rachel MacDonald**, business coach and writer

"*Priestess* is a must read for awakening women everywhere. This book is like a homecoming to your true feminine nature, the part of you that you always felt was there, but it was never given the space to truly soar. You will have tears of remembrance and delight in knowing that everything you have once felt is real and so beautifully powerful. When I think of someone who embodies the energy and the true commitment to living with courage and compassion as a modern-day priestess and sacred leader, I think of Julie Parker."

—**Tracey Spencer**, founder of Lightworkers Academy, author of *Rock Your Light: Lessons for Lightworkers* and *Spiritual Straight Talk to Make Shit Happen*

"What a deeply empowering guide to ancient wisdom! Julie Parker has gifted us with a highly personal and intuitive book that does more than teach us about women spiritual guides of the past and their wisdom, divinity, and heart opening experiences. It also can inspire us to connect with our own power and to the truth of who we are by remembering that our true calling can ignite our spiritual growth and allow us to reclaim our feminine healing gifts."

—**Myriam Llano,** founder of Divine Renewal

"I deeply loved *Priestess*. Beginning with a little history, context and inspiration, Julie sets the scene for what it means to be a powerful, inclusive, sovereign priestess in a world crying out for grounded, loving and aware spiritual leadership. This book is a call to action, a torch to our shadows, permission to be, and an illumination of why this work is so important. It is also a celebration of all that it is to identify as a Woman, in all our divine and complex diversity. I sincerely hope *Priestess* finds her way into the hands of all who identify with or are curious about this courageous, fierce, graceful and humbling journey of the modern-day priestess."

—**Rebecca Coldicutt,** founder of Rebel Starseeds

"Julie walks the priestess path with shining integrity and devotion. Her words are both affirming and rousing. This work is the warmest of invitations to Remember the sacred leader you are and the sacred gifts you embody every day, for which the world hungers."

—**Grace Funk,** founder of Priestess Your Life

# PRIESTESS

*Ancient Spiritual Wisdom*
FOR MODERN SACRED WOMEN

JULIE PARKER

the kind press

Copyright © 2020 Julie Parker

First published by the kind press, 2020

All rights reserved. No part of this book may be reproduced, stored in a retrieval system or transmitted in any form or by any means, electronic, mechanical photocopying, recording, or otherwise, without written permission from the author and publisher.

This publication contains the opinions and ideas of its author. It is intended to provide helpful and informative material on the subjects addressed in the publication. While the publisher and author have used their best efforts in preparing this book, the material in this book is of the nature of general comment only. It is sold with the understanding that the author and publisher are not engaged in rendering medical advice or any other kind of personal professional service in the book. In the event that you use any of the information in this book for yourself, the author and the publisher assume no responsibility for your actions.

Cataloguing-in-Publication entry is available from the National Library Australia.

NATIONAL LIBRARY OF AUSTRALIA

ISBN 978-0-6485917-8-8 (Paperback)
ISBN 978-0-6485917-9-5 (Ebook)

For the two before and the one after,
Nana, Mum, Sinéad.
For all that you were and are.

# Contents

ACKNOWLEDGEMENTS  *xxi*
INTRODUCTION  *xxiv*
ABOUT PRIESTESS  *xxviii*

## PART I
## HER LIVING, HER RETREATING, HER RISING
1

MAMA KNOWS EVERYTHING
8

GODDESSES, GODDESSES, EVERYWHERE
10

HER HANDMAIDENS
12

THEY CAME ON HORSES
14

SHE'S BACK
17

BUT AM I ACTUALLY ONE
19

THEY'LL THINK I'VE LOST IT
22

THE REAL WORK
24

RUBBER STAMP ME STAT!
26

DO WE NEED A SMOKE MACHINE?
28

IS SHE YOU?
30

| xiii

# PART II
## PRIESTESSES PAST TO PRESENT
### 33

MESOPOTAMIAN AND SUMERIAN PRIESTESSES
38

PRIESTESSES OF ÇATAL HÜYÜK
40

HEMET-NETJER
41

GOD'S WIFE OF AMUN
43

THE ELEUSINIAN MYSTERY PRIESTESSES
45

PRIESTESSES OF ARTEMIS
47

THE MELISSAI
49

PRIESTESSES OF ATHENA
50

THE PYTHIA
51

THE VESTAL PRIESTESSES
53

CELTIC PRIESTESSES
55

VÖLUR
57

MAYAN PRIESTESSES
59

MOCHE PRIESTESSES
61

MAMBOS
63

SANTERAS
65

## PART III
## POWER PRIESTESSES
## 67

ENHEDUANNA
71

ENNIGALDI-NANNA
73

HATSHEPSUT
75

ONOMARIS
77

CHRYSIS
79

BOUDICCA
80

VELEDA
82

FIDELM
83

MARY MAGDALENE
84

QUEEN HIMIKO
86

ACONIA FABIA PAULINA
88

BRIGID
89

DAHIA AL-KAHINA
91

MARIE LAVEAU
92

NEHANDA CHARWE NYAKASIKANA
94

FERMINA GÓMEZ PASTRANA
96

## PART IV
## THE INNER CALLING AND BEING
## 99

GUIDE ME, GODDESS
104

THE GREAT WORK
107

LEARNING FROM THE MONKEY
110

BEING PERFECTLY IMPERFECT
114

YOUR JUDGY PANTS DON'T FIT ANYMORE
117

ARE YOU REALLY STRAIGHT?
119

DON'T BE AFRAID OF THE DARK
122

BEYOND LOVE AND LIGHT
126

THE FEAR OF FEAR
129

OUR STORIES OF LONELINESS
132

THE GODDESS SEES ALL
136

WHO STOLE MY FLOWER CROWN?
138

I'M SO SORRY
141

ALIGNMENT
143

YOU FIRST, PRIESTESS
145

HER FREQUENCY, YOUR POWER
147

TINGLY TRINKETS
149

THERE IS NO ROAD MAP
151

YOU KNOW WHAT TO DO
153

# PART V
# LIVING EMBODIED
## 155

SACREDNESS EVERY DAY
159

GOING BACK
161

TAKE ME TO THE ALTAR
164

PASSIONATE PRAYING
166

INTUITION IGNITION
168

MUM'S CALLING
171

THE WHEELS OF THE YEAR GO ROUND AND ROUND
174

LUNA LOVE
180

LIVING ILLUMINATED
183

A BLEEDING SHAME
187

YOUR BLOOD IS BEAUTIFUL
190

BLOODY RITES
192

IT'S INEVITABLE
197

DEATH BECOMES YOU
200

CELEBRATING YOU
203

YOU'RE A WILD ONE
206

SISTER HEALING
209

BEING IN BODY
212

ANAM CARA
215

## PART VI
## YOUR PRIESTESS GIFTS
### 217

THE RITUAL PRIESTESS
222

THE CEREMONIAL PRIESTESS
224

THE BEAUTIFIER PRIESTESS
226

THE VEIL-LIFTER PRIESTESS
228

THE GATHERER AND SPACE-HOLDER PRIESTESS
230

THE PERFORMER AND ARTIST PRIESTESS
232

THE DIVINER PRIESTESS
234

THE HEALER PRIESTESS
236

THE EARTH-WHISPERER PRIESTESS
238

## PART VII
## SACRED LEADERSHIP
## 241

ARE YOU TALKING TO ME?
246

THE SACRED PART
249

LET'S RIDE A NEW (OLD) WAVE
252

BEYOND DREAMING
255

THERE'S NO DENYING IT
258

POWER AND PRIVILEGE
261

TRUE LOVE AND CONNECTION
264

PROTECTING HER, HONOURING THEM
267

ARE YOU ALL IN?
270

YOU ARE YOUR PURPOSE
273

YOUR LIFE IS YOUR LEGACY
276

NOTES  *280*
GODDESS GLOSSARY  *288*
BIBLIOGRAPHY  *290*
INDEX  *295*

# Acknowledgements

The writing of a book like *Priestess* is not something that happens in isolation, even though it can feel at times that the writing process is a solitary one.

*Priestess* is a co-creation of love, inspiration and shared wisdom from so many people, lands and experiences that have touched my life. All have left an imprint on my heart and this book.

I firstly give thanks to the traditional owners of the land where *Priestess* has chiefly been written (Melbourne), the Wurundjeri people of the Kulin Nation, and pay my respects to their elders past, present and emerging. I also extend gratitude to the people of other lands where *Priestess* has been penned, including the Wathaurong people of the Kulin nation (Ballarat), the Arakwal people of the Bundjalung nation (Byron Bay), the Musqueam, Squamish and Tsleil-Waututh First Nations People of Canada (Vancouver), the mystical lands of Avalon and the highlands of Scotland, and the fae-inspired countryside of Ireland. I am eternally grateful for the deep inspiration of the Great Mother who has held me as I have written in each of these places.

Thank you Isabelle Aouad for all your assistance in the research aspects of *Priestess* which have made her so robust. I am grateful for all your incredible fact finding and mystery unveiling.

To my editor and publisher Natasha Gilmour, thank you for holding *Priestess* with such loving hands when I arrived to you somewhat bruised. You knew Her from the very first moment and what I hoped She would do. Thank you for your belief in me and this creation, and to Jasmine Phillips for making Her look and feel so lush.

To the many extraordinary women who have inspired my path of learning about my ancestry, colonialism, white supremacy and social justice, including Desiree Adaway, Ericka Hines, Jessica Fish, Leesa Renee Hall and Sonali Fiske, my gratitude for the work you bring to the world continues to unfold. My special thanks also to Sharyn Holmes for your searing love and lens and how you inspired me to make *Priestess* a better book on all levels. You are a true warrior priestess and I am honoured to know you and be inspired by your work.

For igniting and helping me continue to unfold my path of sacred leadership, I thank the many incredible priestesses I have personally worked with over many years now, including Ariel Spilsbury, Kalila Sofia, L'Erin Alta, Molly Remer, Lauri Ann Lumby, Dr Tjanara Goreng Goreng, Grace Funk, Nymh Fox Harper and Jane Hardwicke Collings.

The love of cherished sisterhood runs deep in *Priestess* and I give loving thanks to Yvette Luciano, Megan Dalla-Camina, Rachel MacDonald, Kate Byrne, Amanda Daley, Tara Bliss, Dr Ezzie Spencer and Angela

Simson for all your holding of *Priestess* and my heart as She unfolded.

To my most 'beautiful' girls, women, mavens and beloved team of Liz Deanna, Johanna Parker, Jade McKenzie, Ellie Swift, Sammie Fleming, Leana Mullane, and Laura Banks, I give thanks every day for the inspiration and love you gift me with. Thank you for all you are.

To my heart sister and fellow temple space holder of Priestess Temple School, Sora Surya No, you are on every page of this book. Your love and sisterhood are one of the greatest gifts of my life and I thank the Goddess for Her infinite spark of light in bringing our lives together.

To all the amazing pioneering women of my family, especially my beloved mum, and nieces Olivia and Rachael, I hold such hope and love in our hearts for all that we have been and come from, and where we may go.

To my stepdaughter Sinéad, your kindness, humility and thoughtfulness inspire me every day. I have thought of you so often as the words of *Priestess* have been written.

My Viking Englishman and husband Glenn, thank you for loving me. A book such as *Priestess* needs love in every word to truly be carried out to the world and that is your legacy in these pages.

To the Great Mother, Goddess, God and Universe who have blessed me with this life; my deepest prayers of gratitude, respect and love. Thank you for allowing me to live a life of my choosing and create *Priestess* as a part of my soul gifts.

# Introduction

When we are exploring the world of women's spiritual leadership, and the world of the Priestess, it is vital to note that history is chiefly written by men and is therefore often diminishing of, or completely erasing of women.

Welcome to the patriarchy.

What may—or even did—take place is unlikely to be recorded well or even at all when it comes to the role women once played as spiritual leaders and priestesses. And if something was recorded, it was often deliberately inaccurate in an attempt to subjugate women and deny them power and agency, especially in the area of spirituality, which was so important to the lives of people in pre-Christian times. The research and evidence in some places and from some cultures is robust, but in others it is sketchy, biased or non-existent. And while there have been moments where I have felt an intense longing to make claim to certain practices or ways of the ancient priestesses, if there has not been sound evidence for this—or at the very least a strong argument that could be made for it being truth—I have not included it in *Priestess*.

Throughout *Priestess* you will note that sometimes it may not be clear whether a woman and priestess referred to is actually a real person. Where there are parts of someone's life that are *not* fully known, there are competing stories, or she may be mythical in character, this is noted. I then encourage you to allow your heart to guide you in what you choose to believe about her humanness or otherwise.

I have seen many people make claims about certain priestess or goddess practices that I have not been able to substantiate, even with extensive research, for the purposes of *Priestess*. Does this mean that they may not have happened or that someone's particular belief is not true? Not necessarily. It may be and feel very true to them on a personal level, but just not be able to be explicitly substantiated in any way. And while I can speak of my own personal experience, I cannot to anyone else's, and therefore within these pages I have stayed in the lane of what is researched and as factual as possible.

When I use the word 'woman' in *Priestess*, I mean woman and woman identifying. I do not believe that someone has to be a cisgendered woman or wholly identify as one to feel the priestess calling or commit to being one. This is especially the case when so many of the goddesses and gods that priestesses worship and worshipped were gender fluid. Therefore, it is entirely hypocritical for me and the priestess community worldwide to be anything but gender inclusive. Any cries of 'if you're not born a woman, you're not a woman' fall into the transphobic and exclusionary bin for me and do nothing more than keep this work out of the hearts and minds of extraordinary people who have so much to offer it.

There may be priestesses by name or lineage whom I do not mention in this book that are important to you. I've chosen to write about the ones I am most inspired by and also have been able to find factual and non-conflicting information about. It excites me to think that in years to come there could be many more priestess lineages uncovered that we know little or nothing about now.

Throughout time, the priestess has been known by many names and titles. Banduri, oracle, seer, prophetess, völva, entu, mambo, midwife, druidess, healer, witch and more. There are also different types of priestesses within different lineages that carry different names. Might some of them, if they were here with us now, believe that 'priestess' was an appropriate title for them? Maybe, but also maybe not. What I am sure they would be, though, is proud to have their work and devotion noted so far beyond their lives, regardless of the title given to them.

Priestesses come from so many different cultures, religions and lineages that gaining agreement on exactly who they were and now are, and what they did and now do, isn't possible. Some are very focused on earth-based traditions or devoted to a particular goddess, and others are more connected to particular healing practices and so much more. We all have our own definition, cultural lineage and devoted spiritual practices, and I think it's vital we not get into a binary of 'You can't be this if ...' or 'You can only be that if ...'.

I'm so grateful to you for holding this book in your hands. That means it's likely you know a lot more about me than I do about you. I do not know your cultural background, age or spiritual beliefs and practices. When I mention goddesses and practices of certain cultures, they may not resonate with you, or even if they do, they may not be acceptable for you to use in a way that is not culturally appropriate. I encourage you to live as priestesses in the world in a way that is aligned with your own cultural background and the goddesses, gods, beliefs and practices that are a part of that. You will be richer in your own spiritual life for it and leave to other cultures those practices that are sacred and precious to them. My cultural lineage is predominantly from England, Scotland, Ireland and Wales, with my remaining heritage from Iberia, Greece, Italy and the Balkans.

Trust yourself as you read these pages. Listen to the deepest part of your soul voice in what is true for you. Love beyond any egoic voice that arises that says you are not worthy or that you cannot call upon and connect with your deepest spiritual wisdom within, and what the path of the priestess may be to you. You are a sovereign being. This life is yours to do with as you are most deeply and powerfully called. And that includes a life as a priestess if you desire.

I do not have the answers to what being a priestess may mean to you. I have only my own. I have been publicly speaking about and embracing my life as a priestess for six years. It feels in many ways so small, such a tiny part of my five decades thus far. However, I was called to the spiritual path of the goddess as a girl, and even though I failed to understand what that meant then, my life as it has unfolded has seen me do exactly as She has called me to do. As you skim, dance or lovingly thumb through these pages, know that you have the answers to what being a priestess means to you within you already.

*Priestess* is to inspire your awakening or continued unfolding as a spiritual and sacred leader.

**Where you go from here, only the Divine and you together can know.**

# About Priestess

My wish for you is that *Priestess* becomes a beloved guide and companion as you journey through the incredible life you have been given. A guide that you use for spiritual inspiration, comfort and exploration as you find out what it means to be a modern spiritual leader and priestess in today's world. On your own terms.

Your life and existence are sacred to me. As you hold this book in your hands, I want you to know that I see you for all that you are and all that you are becoming. Such is the way of the priestess. A recognition of sister to sister that believes in your infinite light and capacity.

*Priestess* will first take you back in time to when women—your ancestors—were holy and revered, and where priestesses were known to be the loving messengers of the goddesses and gods on earth. You will learn about ancient priestess collectives from lands such as Sumer, Egypt, Greece and Peru, and be inspired by known priestesses from around the world including Germany, Japan, Zimbabwe and Cuba.

*Priestess* then becomes personal and she will guide you to ... *you*. To your inner world, calling and being, where She will encourage you to open up to all that you already see and honour within yourself and all that you do not. Most of all that you do not. For that is where your untold and as yet unseen magic, healing and wholeness truly dwell. You will then explore what it means to live as a priestess for yourself every day and lean deeply and lovingly into your sacred gifts as one.

Finally, *Priestess* issues you a call to action, a call that asks you to honour your sacred leader within and consider with deep commitment how it is that you will use your spiritual gifts to create radical change, inspire love and action, and uplift those around you in meaningful ways. It is a call to service that only you can fulfil.

Along the way, it is my hope that you will come to see yourself in these pages as a sacred spiritual being whose precious life is a gift and has such great meaning.

**Go well, sister.
I hold you in my heart as you step into the world of *Priestess*.
I walk beside you every step of the way.**

# PART I

# Her Living, Her Retreating, Her Rising

Imagine a time when women were holy.
Revered. Honoured. Sacred.

Once we were warriors. And healers. And guides.
And the embodied voice of the goddess.

Once we were priestesses.

*We served in grand temples built in honour of the goddesses and in the simplest of dwellings in our local community.*

*We called upon our oracular skills and intuition in service to royalty and our neighbour.*

*We led powerful ceremonies and rituals watched by hundreds and seen by none.*

*We gathered women in circles, honouring the moon and seasons and cycles of the Great Mother Goddess.*

*We wove magic with herbs, wounds and deep longings of the soul.*

*We were joyous songstresses, seamstresses, dancers and poets.*

*We were fierce fighters on bloody battlefields and powerful political influencers behind velvet curtains.*

*We were honoured and known by name for thousands of years into the future and passed through the veil to the underground unknown.*

*We were of and for the people and we were both known and unknown.*

**The time of the ancient priestess was a great time for women. We were leaders, protectresses, guides and lights.**

The closer we creep to modern times, however, the more evidence of the patriarchy we see; things significantly change for women and our spiritual selves and lives. And we are shown that the history of the priestess is in so many ways the history of women.

As we move through a world today that is steeped in kyriarchy, so many of us have an intense longing to know ourselves beyond layered oppressions, driving external forces and the pervasive opinion of the status quo. To know the depths of our soul and the beautiful mystery of our divinity felt only when in communion with our truest self. To honour the magic and wisdom of those before us and who we have emerged as time and time, life and life again. To transcend our fear. To commune with the earth as our life source and feel the depths of Her language, energy and wildness as a reflection of our most free self. To know we are loved and held by the Universe, Goddess, God, our ancestors, allies and land, in ways that allow us to see our magnificent wholeness.

It is a calling that asks us to be seen as we are now, and with vulnerability and care, who we desire to become. A calling that sees us as held and upheld by the women before us and the women around us and after us.

We are all holy when seen through the eyes of love. All leaders when led by compassion. All priestesses when a decision is made to live in deep spiritual service to oneself and others.

Women have always been the spiritual leaders the world most needs us to be.

We are creators of hope. Conduits of spirit. Holders of magic. Messengers of love. Priestesses.

Priestesses of past and now of present too.

**We were.**
**We are.**
**We always will be.**

# Mama Knows Everything

In ancient times, people truly believed that their Mother knew everything.

While people had a birth mother—that they may or may not have known, just as it is today—their spiritual Mother, life provider and protector was the greatest and most honoured goddess of all. She was, and still is, known as the Great Mother, Mother Nature, Mother Earth, the Great Goddess, the Great Mother Goddess, Gaia, Pachamama, Papatūānuku, Akna, Papahānaumoku and so many more names according to time and one's culture and spiritual beliefs. I honour all Her names but call Her the Great Mother.

Life was held and entirely influenced by Her on a daily basis.

Her fertility and bloom, softness and ferocity, and fire and storm were the driving force of life. When crops would be planted and harvested. When to move. When to stay. What could be gently taken from Her. What was to be given back. The magic of Her plants, herbs and medicine to heal the sick. Her life source of food, shelter and protection. The cycle of Her seasons marking birth, growth, decay, death and rebirth. And Her endless source of inspiration and beauty.

And women were seen to be a reflection of this great beauty and power and Her cyclic wisdom as well. Women were the human embodiment of Her: powerful, wise, capable, strong, gentle, fierce, giving, connected, cyclic beings.

And as such, women experienced a divine sense of safety, belonging and love for their place and roles in the world.

# Goddesses, Goddesses Everywhere

In ancient times both goddesses and gods were widely worshipped, but the goddess held a very special place in the hearts and spiritual lives of people.

The Mesopotamians, Babylonians, Egyptians, Greeks, Romans and many more ancient cultures believed in goddesses and gods as higher supernatural beings who created and maintained order throughout the world and Universe. Each had a special sphere of influence. No one person, goddess or god was thought to be able to provide for someone's entire life and spiritual needs. If you were experiencing challenges in your romantic life you went to the goddess of love, if you were worried about your safety you called upon the goddess of protection, if you wanted to recover from an illness you called upon the goddess of health.

More than 20,000 years ago, images of goddesses appeared extensively throughout the world. Statues and cave paintings of figures with breasts, some pregnant, and many with circles and spirals representing their cyclic nature, were prominent. These depictions were once thought to be just fertility symbols; now they are widely believed to be representations of the Mother Goddess as the great creator and source of all life. The goddesses were also represented in animal form including as a dove, owl, bear, doe and bee, and prominently identified with the life-giving aspects of water, plants and the moon.

As living representations of the goddess, women in these times were seen and honoured as powerful life-givers without whom humanity could not exist. It was a time when the reflection of women as Cybele or Isis or Demeter meant she was Divine. When all parts of Her were grace, beauty and softness, and also power, strength and fury. No part of a woman was unloved or seen to be less than man or other women.

> **Women gained connection and love from worshipping the goddess as themselves.**
> **They saw themselves in Her and believed She did in them.**

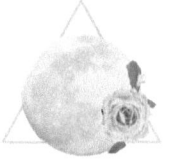

# Her Handmaidens

At a time when the goddess was so honoured, women who walked the earth were seen as Her divine conduits and messengers. Direct reflections of their strength, beauty and power, women as handmaidens of the goddess were Her priestesses.

Bringers of love, hope, protection, second sight, healing and a higher connection to self, Priestesses supported people in their communities to be in greater connection with their true selves, with each other, and with the goddesses—and sometimes gods—that guided every aspect of their life.

In ancient Mesopotamia and Sumer, priestesses administered both religious and medical services. The priestesses of Çatal Hüyük were conductors of powerful rituals, and those of ancient Egypt, Greece and Rome were revered as some of the most prominent, powerful and important members of their societies. Celtic priestesses were mediators, ceremonialists and warrior trainers, and Mayan priestesses were renowned ritualists and midwives.

The role of the priestess was held in the highest regard and without suspicion or question. They were seen as vital members of their communities, responsible for the spiritual health and wellbeing of those around them; wayshowers for people to honour the messages and desires of the goddess and gods according to the seasons, moon cycles, fertility and survival.

Far from subservient or dominated, priestesses in many cultures of the past were key political, economic, medical, educational and spiritual leaders. They held entire communities together with their grace, intuitive abilities, healing skills and deep abilities to connect to oneself and each other.

**They were the ties that bound in the most profound ways.**

**Until they weren't.**

# They Came On Horses

Everything changed for the world of the priestess, and therefore for women, with the global spread of warring nomadic tribes and their belief in only male gods, and eventually, one male God.[1] The systemic and oppressive regime of the patriarchy began. And flourished.[2]

War, brutality, colonisation and denial of goddesses and the role of the Great Mother as spiritual life force and protector came to be. As did the denial of women as sovereign beings. And sisterhood, community and connection on egalitarian terms.

The cataclysmic shift began about 6,000 to 8,000 years ago, when violent raiders on horseback stormed throughout the Middle East, Europe and Asia, moving around the fringes of stable agricultural societies as nomadic marauders. Organised in male hierarchies of priests and warriors, they worshipped only male gods. Annihilating the partnership model of goddess-centred society, they overturned it to one steeped in control and conquest, supported by materials such as bronze and iron to make weapons. Peaceful agrarian cultures could offer little resistance.

The seeds of war, colonisation, slavery, capitalism and animal and environmental destruction were planted. And grew. And with them came the widespread subjugation of women. No longer seen as divine and powerful reflections of goddesses whose myths and powers were dishonoured, women found their place in the world violently and suddenly changed forever, and only in some ways have we seen it recovered since.

Women came to be seen as the property of men, existing for their pleasure, to carry on their name, help them colonise, plunder and own land, be forced into domestication and held up as examples of what was sinful. Their lives were defined almost solely under the meaning of what it meant to be a wife, and their virginity and sexuality seen as something which required simultaneous protection and controlling. Under the direct and societally sanctioned control of their fathers and husbands, women held little to no autonomy.

It is hard to imagine the utter devastation this must have brought into the lives of women and all they held so close. An almost total loss of liberty in all areas of their being—physical, sexual, spiritual and more. Their birthright as sovereign beings questioned and quashed. Their skills, gifts and leadership denied. Their wildness and free spirit tamed. Their belief in and connection to the Great Mother severed, and with it, all that they knew of creation, birth, life, growth, death and rebirth. And with this seismic shift came thousands of years of violent and oppressive punishment, torture and rape, as well as trials, hangings and murder, often connected to their spiritual beliefs and practices and the threat women were seen to be to the new patriarchal and religious hierarchy.

And women's connection to each other was shattered as well. Forced into private family structures and away from collaborative community, dominated by suspicion and control, forced to judge, spy and see each other as competition. Woman-to-woman connection and sisterhood was ripped apart. With ongoing consequences that we still experience today.

**They tried to bury us. No doubt.**

**And in many ways, they did.**

In the rich, cool, dark underbelly of the Great Mother where we have slowly waited for it to be not just our time, but time for all of us, *again*.

# She's Back

The Divine Feminine, spirit of the goddesses, power of women as spiritual leaders—as priestesses—has never truly died.

**Denied and silenced, yes.
Dead? Never.**

She has lived on in billions of us who have resisted, simply by surviving and being here now to witness the time of Her rebirth as our own. Where we can tap into a loving curiosity of what it means to be a spiritual leader today and be committed to moving through any fear that may come with that. To know what it means to be whole and sovereign. To move back into right relation with the Great Mother, sisterhood and community. And to harness our power and privilege to challenge white supremacy, racism, heteronormativity, ableism, exclusion, and more, to our fullest extent.

Women are reclaiming their birthrights as spiritual and sacred leaders. Refusing to be told there is only one way or path to soul belonging and earthly living. Refusing to honour the notion that only men hold the mysteries and spirit of the Universe and are conduits to speak for them. Refusing to not see and honour their gifts and magic for themselves and others. Refusing to not believe that they have the power to influence change in the most profound ways at individual, community and collective levels.

Women are falling in love with their spiritual selves, divinity and leadership all over again. As we as a collective of human souls need them to. More than ever before. And with this love we become witness to the re-emergence and rising of priestesses as they unfurl, stand tall and emerge as the seers, healers and space holders they truly are.

> They are saying, 'Yes! This is me now, what I am called to be. I am a priestess. I feel the ancientness of this in my heart and bones. I will not be denied, nor will I deny others. There is work to be done where I long to see myself as whole. Where I challenge systems of oppression with my righteous anger, power and love. This is a new me that is also a reflection and honouring of the old me and all that I have come to be right now. I will not deny my leadership or my longing to know myself as a spiritual being.
>
> 'I have taken my time for the task ahead to become the priestess and spiritual leader I know the world needs right now.
>
> 'I am back.
>
> I am here.'

PRIESTESS

# But Am I Actually One?

The first time I heard the word 'priestess', I had what can only be described as an embodied spiritual experience. And my life was forever changed.

I had always been embracing of my own spirituality, way beyond my Christian upbringing, where the thing I loved most about church was singing rousing hymns. Growing up on a working farm, I was in touch with the beauty of the Great Mother every day, even though I was often the family member who was more indoors, cooking for hungry farmers, shearers and animal tenders, than I was outdoors. The vegetables, fruits and herbs I worked with in our tiny kitchen came from somewhere, and that somewhere was our garden and orchard. Almost daily, my hands were in the ground, or picking up eggs, and gently washing, preparing and serving food we had grown and cared for from seed.

And I was deeply connected to a wider, higher and deeper belief in something beyond myself from childhood. You do not grow up watching bees collect pollen like the lightworkers they are, spiders weaving spellbound magic, roses blooming in severe drought, baby animals being born in wild storms, and live on land that gives to you every day, and not know that greater wisdom and power is afoot than what you can see with your eyes. And through the power of the Great Mother that all is connected.

What is this if not your spirituality?

A debater, speaker and writer as a young girl with a very dominant Leo star sign, I also held no doubt that my future as a woman was one that would be of my own making. And be of service. I held little regard for rules that I felt caged my female friends and I at our tiny country high school. And went into battle more than once when my fire refused to allow me to be silent. I won the battle—together with every other girl in my school in a fierce uprising—for students with intellectual disabilities to remain in mainstream class. I lost to being able to join the cricket team. You win some. You lose some. You move on.

This word that was to become an opening and calling of priestess, however, was like nothing I had ever experienced. A divine woman I was interviewing for an article, Sarah Jenks, shared with me that one of the greatest teaching paths in her life had been that of the priestess. In poor interviewing form I lost my place with her instantly. I could hear Sarah talking but was no longer listening. I found myself instantly wrapped in a cloak of goosy tingles, an expanding heat in my chest and a deep stirring in my womb space that I had never felt before.

Sarah, simply through her own presence as a powerful priestess and expressing her truth, had opened a portal for me. It had always been there but was clearly waiting for the right time for me to access it. It was no coincidence that it opened at the end of a period of time in my life where I had come through a searing fire of relationship grief and loss, deeply challenging physical health issues and depression. I had never worked so profoundly on my own inner healing and call to wholeness.

*It was my time.*

After wrapping up the interview and thanking Sarah for her time as calmly as I could, I instantly found myself down a rabbit hole—*Alice in Wonderland* style—soaking up all I could about the world of the priestess. Who she was. What she did. Her connection to goddess and the Great Mother. I became a student again, and in a hot heartbeat a leader of my own spiritual self. I sought out teachers and guides to support my journey in all forms. They both came to me and I went to them. And we journey still.

I then began to piece together the wispy strands of thread in my family line and what this path may have meant for us and for me now. I found healers, carers, nurturers, community leaders, pioneers, wild adventurers and stewardesses of the land. Holders of space. And hands. And hearts. My line. My women.

**Priestesses all in their own right.**

**Yes. They really were one.**

**Yes. I really am one.**

# They'll Think I've Lost It

Knowing and coming to believe that you are something like a priestess sounds a little bit, or even more than a little bit, lovely, but can in fact be deeply scary and even threatening to your own sense of self and safety.

After my initial cocooned months of exploring what being a priestess meant for me, especially how I was being called to heal myself further and be in deeper service to others, my ego started to rise, and with it what I can only describe as spiritual anxiety and displacement. *What will people think? I am going to be grilled for this. How can I explain something I still don't fully understand? Are people going to think this is something to do with the Catholic church and I've converted? Is someone going to ask me if I'm becoming a nun? Am I becoming a nun? Will it be expected I give up my business? How can I possibly attempt to be heard or understood here? I can't. They won't. We have a problem.* As a result, my smaller self, initially, and very loudly, told me to keep this whole priestess 'thing' quiet or I could jeopardise or even lose everything that I had created and built for myself, including my business, relationships and more. And besides that, I didn't even know what I was doing anyway. In the slightest. And so, mouth, *shut it*.

And then one seemingly innocuous day, after more than a year of deep spiritual journeying, I said the words 'I am a priestess' to a room full of extraordinary entrepreneurs in—of all holy (or unholy!) places—New York City. A searing and brilliant talk given by master coach and maven, Tanya Geisler, about the imposter complex had us traversing a conversation on stage about owning one's power, claiming one's gifts through fear and living on purpose. And it just came, entirely unplanned, to be spoken.

No one, least of all me, died or fell to the floor, then or afterwards.

And Tanya simply said in reply, 'Well, of course, you are.'

And it was out.

# The Real Work

So, no one died or collapsed once my priestess self publicly emerged, but She—I—still had much to traverse. My egoic resistance continued, despite the fact that on the whole I received loving support and thoughtful questions as to what a priestess actually was. I was working on that at the time and still am. I began to search for 'hard' evidence for this claim and if it was truly okay for me to not just see myself as a priestess, privately, but to claim my place as one in the wider world. I questioned my abilities, my divinity, my personal authority, my sovereignty, and what this was really all about. What I was all about.

Was I grasping for a title to make myself feel spiritually big, like I somehow knew more than everyone else? To have others see me as more enlightened. Be taken more seriously. Where is the evidence that it is acceptable and okay and even *right* to call myself a priestess?

And so the real initial work of this path presented itself to me. I presented it to myself. The deeper inner journey that all priestesses must go on came to be. And in doing so we danced. My ego. My soul. My fear. My intuition. My self-loathing. My self-love. My frailty. My strength. My humanity. My divinity.

I came to know myself as I never had before, and that even though to some it felt like 'all of a sudden' I was a priestess, I wasn't. For many years, unknown to only those closest to me, I was unfolding, learning, being guided, taught, remembering, dreaming and working as a soul-fuelled spiritual leader in my own way. I just didn't know or see it as such.

And maybe I would have gone my entire life not realising and nothing would have been different from how I showed up and served in the world. Just like so many women before us who have lived deeply as priestesses and possibly not realised it. Like so many women before us who have had gifts of healing, gathering and spiritual leadership and not been able to be known or seen for their true power. Or even the generations of women before us who have simply never known their true power as woman suppressed beneath societal, familial and religious expectations that have forced them to be small and silent.

No hard, scientific or certificate-like evidence came to me, but rather an integration of my own knowing, ancestral wisdom, deep healing and continuing to be in service to others brought forth a quiet knowing and spiritual belonging to myself. To myself as priestess. That I was to walk as one through life and continually unfold my own conditioning so that I may see out my soul's purpose in this human body and potentially, for those curious and willing, support them to do the same. In doing so, in continuing to do so, I came to learn that when we claim or reclaim a priestess path for ourselves now, we do so for all women before us who may not have been able to as well. I believe they are watching us, feeling us, seeing us. And willing us on.

**In every part of who we are and who we are becoming. To heal all that has come before.**

**And all that will come after.**

# Rubber Stamp Me Stat!

My journey continued, and while no priestess certificate in luscious curly font fell from the goddess heavens to say I was one, still I searched for a rubber stamp of legitimacy.

Okay, so I am. But how do I 'prove' this?

I came to learn about the muddy, and at times, painful path that is unravelling oneself from patriarchal conditioning and coming to believe in one's own spiritual gifts. With no validation required. The more I embraced myself, the more I claimed my path as a priestess, led by my own wisdom and longing. And that gradually, and with reverence, any reading, mentoring, collective training, circles, experiences and remembrances I committed to, I did so *not* in search for legitimacy, but in search for myself and how I could be in the deepest level of service as a priestess in the world.

There will never be agreement about whether or not one needs to be trained or ordained as a priestess. There are those who say that if you have to say you are a priestess then you are not one. There are those who say that you are not one until you are ordained in a modern mystery school or developed lineage. There are those who say you are not a priestess unless you are devoted entirely and openly to a goddess for life. Some claim that as a priestess you must be in a temple space regularly. Some that you cannot be one unless you come from a blood line. And there are those who say you are not a priestess unless you are in a collective that has a common purpose.

Much of this binary thinking is to me simply more patriarchal conditioning. Bloodline? Really? We're not talking about being the descendants of a royal family here! And let's not even dive into those as oppressive regimes. That if you say you are one then you aren't? Talk about a convenient way to hide and take the beauty of humility way too detrimentally far. I could go on.

There is no rubber stamp here and no one path for us all. Only you can unfold the journey that will lead you to the mystery of your soul and how you are meant to show up in the world as a priestess. How you will commit. How you will exercise your faith. How you will honour your own need to heal and grow. How you will honour the divinity in others. How you will revel in sisterhood. How you will lead in spiritual service.

It is not something to say you are if you know you are not, or not committed to unfolding. It is not something to claim without due reverence. It is not something to hold onto if deep resonance does not come. It is also not something to be bathed in snobbery or a patriarchal cloak about. Or to try to place that on someone else.

I have heard my priestess sister, Sora Surya No, say many times that there is no destination one ever arrives at, and that your initiation as a priestess begins once you make a decision to step onto a path as one.

**And so it is.**

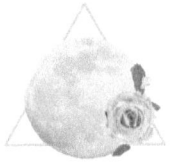

# Do We Need a Smoke Machine?

By the time I was wholly owning of my priestess path—and writing about it on social media and in my own writing and conversations—things had shifted for me. I was no longer afraid.

While I cannot be fully sure my priestess path was the reason, I did lose followers and people in my life the more I spoke about my spiritual journey. I also gained many more, and an even deeper relationship with others that was, and continues to be, beyond beautiful. My spiritual world and those in it opened up to be wider and deeper than it ever had before.

My husband, Glenn, noticed a change in me, and as he always has, held my excitement for the unfolding of women's spiritual leadership I felt a groundswell in my heart for. I spoke excitedly with him about how women—if they chose and it was right for them—could tap into deeper powers of their own knowing and leadership like we had never seen before. One day, I told him I was going to go live on social media and talk about this more for the first time. With whip-like precision he asked, 'Do we need to buy a smoke machine?' Flying around to face him with faux indignation, but unable to stop laughing, I cried foul for him making fun of me, to which he replied he was only half joking and to not forget my sense of humour and joy on this journey. It opened up a chat between us about his upbringing in the Catholic church and how devoid it was of lightness in every way.

That conversation opened my heart up to a commitment I made at every turn on this path to never get too serious, esoteric or defined when speaking about the path of the priestess. To know that even with all that comes with being a spiritual leader—the inner work, the healing, the deeper calling—that if it cannot eventually be felt in some way with joy, then what is it? Not much.

I'm still not convinced about the smoke machine. But one day for fun and dramatic effect in honour of the goddess. Maybe! If it's good enough for my beloved Priestess of Pop, Stevie Nicks, then it just may be for me too.

# Is She You?

How are you feeling right in this very moment?

Take a moment wherever you are to place your hand over your heart, gently close your eyes and take a deep breath in. And out. In. And out.

Are you sensing a stirring inside you? A longing or remembrance? A calling? Did you maybe feel something deep and significant within before you picked up this book? Do you feel Her within you, strong and true already? Or is She whispering to you right now and seeing if you will heed Her call?

Whatever you may be feeling, if you have read this far and are curious to read on, it is likely that a path as a priestess is calling you in some way. Your curiosity is a beautiful thing and can help ignite courage, momentum, acknowledgement and so much more in you. Where you may go from here is so exciting.

To walk as a priestess in your lifetime is a commitment. You don't put on a flower crown or cape when you step into a sacred circle or a healing session and then whisk it off and you are no longer one. When you are a priestess you are one in every waking moment—and dreaming moment—of your life.

You are a walking vessel of love, presence and guidance. You are committed to loving yourself as a spiritual being with all your emotions, feelings, imperfections and messes as well as your triumphs, deep soul moments and experiences of ecstasy. There is no in between. You commit to the calling and you walk forever in whatever way being a priestess comes forth in you.

**And how may that be?**

**Only you will know, but I hope the rest of your journey with this book will assist you to lovingly find out.**

# PART II

# Priestesses Past to Present

There are collectives of priestesses from ancient worlds and pantheons, through to the times of our great grandmothers and grandmothers, and today, that can teach us so much as spiritual leaders. The powerful roles they undertook. Their love of land, the Great Mother and natural elements. Their belief in their own second sight and healing powers. Their devotion to the goddess.

Today's modern mystery schools are an interpretation of these wisdoms and spiritual practices. And maybe in years to come, the collectives we can be a part of now will be looked upon by future generations as antiquated, as women teleport themselves globally to be in communion with each other!

To deepen my own priestess journey, I have been a part of a number of online and in-person mystery schools and trainings including the 13 Moon Mystery School, School of Shamanic Womancraft, Authentic Freedom Academy, and Brigid's Grove. And now I serve with my priestess sister Sora Surya No in our own Priestess Temple School. Each has given me something special and reverent at a particular time on my priestess path, leading me to a place where I am in service in person to my local community and online to our larger collective as a whole. I know my Celtic grandmothers of hundreds and thousands of years whisper their blessings and words of wisdom in my ears every day. They stand behind me as the women and ancestors I come from.

Priestesses, past to present, will show you that many priestesses across cultures belonged to powerful collectives, serving their communities side by side. Others held a more singular path, but one that was still mostly undertaken with sisters never too far away. And this I feel is one of the greatest callings of the modern priestess: how we honour this path not alone, but with each other, so that we may be of the greatest and deepest spiritual service to the world possible.

# Mesopotamian and Sumerian Priestesses

Sumer was an ancient civilisation, during the Chalcolithic and Early Bronze Age, about 4500 to 1900 BCE, in southern Mesopotamia, which is today southern Iraq and Kuwait.[1]

Priestesses were extraordinarily powerful in Sumerian society and were seen to be the equal of any king for their role as mediators between the gods, goddesses and people. In general, Mesopotamian priests served a male god, and priestesses a goddess, though some priestesses worked in the temples of the gods. They had many duties and responsibilities honouring goddesses such as Inanna and Ereshkigal, for which they received respect, honour and special comforts.

There were two main leadership roles Sumerian priestesses could undertake in Mesopotamian temples. The first was as the high priestess, known as an *entu*, who oversaw the sacred duties of all temple priestesses and priests. This included tasks such as singing, making music, writing hymns, performing purifications and, as the first doctors and dentists of Mesopotamia, treating the sick and injured.[2][3] The second role was as chief administrator of the temple, known as a *sanga*. The sanga was a business role due to Sumerian temples being not only places of worship, but of commercial activity as well. Temples ran trade networks and owned land, and the sanga oversaw all of these operations and employees such as bookkeepers, scribes, guards, messengers and seamstresses.[4]

Young women who wanted to be Sumerian priestesses had to be strong in body and come from a good family. Girls who were thought to show aptitude to be a priestess were given the same education as boys. The priestess training was long and arduous but came with significant reward.[5]

Sumerian priestesses were required to be celibate, but although they could not bear children, they could marry and be a stepmother to their husband's children. However, most priestesses chose to live permanently at the temple serving the goddesses and gods and providing religious and medical services to their communities.

# Priestesses of Çatal Hüyük

Çatal Hüyük was a Neolithic city in Southern Anatolia, modern-day Turkey, which thrived between 7000 and 5000 BCE.[6] Large excavations have found art and artefacts that show ancient society in Çatal Hüyük was egalitarian and that women were not considered subordinate to men in any way.[7]

Temple remains show Çatal Hüyük women as priestesses preparing and conducting rituals that involved music, dance and meditation.[8] Life centred around a Mother Goddess who was simultaneously loved and feared for Her ability to give life and take it away.

Around 4500 BCE the peaceful existence enjoyed by the people of Çatal Hüyük was violently disrupted by the arrival of invading tribes from Indo-Europe who worshipped sky gods.[9] The invasion annihilated the Mother Goddess beliefs of the gentle and equal culture, and a society ruled by hierarchy and a male priesthood took over.

# Hemet-Netjer

The priestesses of ancient Egypt, known as *hemet-netjer* (servants of God), lived in devotion to the gods and goddesses of various temples including the goddesses Isis, Nephthys and Hathor. They performed the same duties and received the same pay as male priests.[10]

The hemet-netjer undertook a variety of functions including maintenance of the temple, astronomy, dream interpretation, and mortuary and funeral rituals. Hemet-netjers who embalmed and mummified corpses were highly respected due to the role they played in guaranteeing the deceased eternal life. Daily temple rituals in honour of the deities had a special focus on ensuring the continued health and fertility of the land and Egyptian people.

Most hemet-netjer positions were part-time and they would serve the temple for a month, three times a year. During this time, they were expected to be ritually pure and bathe numerous times a day while living in the temple complex.[11] For the remainder of the year they lived in their communities.

A hemet-netjer's role was purely to serve the deity she was devoted to. She never administered spiritual counsel to the general population. Sometimes people would come to the temple for medical or financial assistance, or to leave an offering, but it was known that the hemet-netjer chiefly existed to serve the goddess and gods and not them.

# God's Wife of Amun

Women who held the position of God's Wife of Amun were some of the most powerful leaders in ancient Egyptian history. At times equal in status to that of a pharaoh, these priestesses served Amun, who was the God of air and sun. Amun was believed to encompass all aspects of creation and Egyptian life.

Many priestesses served as a God's Wife of Amun over hundreds of years and they were usually the mother, wife or daughter of a king, although some were the daughter of a high priest. Their responsibilities included performing daily rituals—for which they prepared by bathing in a sacred lake—the saying of grace before meals, burning effigies of Amun's enemies, shaking and playing rattles, known as *sistra*, and performing religious rites at ceremonies and festivals.

A God's Wife of Amun had her own income and was also given things such as land, clothing, precious metals, wigs, cosmetics and oil. While she utilised payment given to her to assist in the performing of her priestess duties, the land she was given generated revenue that she could personally keep. Her position was a revered and honoured one and as well as her spiritual duties she was often called upon to share her counsel on matters of politics and state. Some of the most significant priestesses who served as God's Wives of Amun included Nefertari, Hatshepsut and Isis.

The position of God's Wife of Amun slowly diminished after the Persian army invaded Egypt in 525 BCE. Although the Persians respected Egyptian religion and culture on the whole, the position of God's Wife of Amun was abolished and high priests became the only people who served Persian kings. By 285 BCE, worship of Amun had disappeared with the spread of Christianity.

# The Eleusinian Mystery Priestesses

The priestesses of the Eleusinian Mysteries were the secret ritual holders of the mystery school of Eleusis observed from 1600 BCE to 392 CE.[12]

The Mysteries held each year at Eleusis in Greece were based on a symbolic reading of the story of the goddesses Demeter and Persephone. This reading provided initiates with a vision of the afterlife so powerful that it changed the way they saw the world and their place in it forever. Virtually every important thinker and writer in antiquity was an initiate of the Mysteries, including Plato and Socrates. Initiates came to recognise that their lives had an eternal purpose and they were not just living to die. This belief in reincarnation provided people with a sense of peace that they would have another chance to experience life on earth in other forms.

It is likely that the Mysteries were influenced by Egyptian religious beliefs which understood death as a transition to another phase of existence, not the end of one's life. Time was considered cyclical, not linear, and one could recognise patterns of the universe through the changing seasons and understand that, just as trees, grass, and flowers died in one season and returned to life in another, so would human beings.

The rituals were closed down by the Christian Emperor Theodosius in 392 CE, as he saw the ancient rites as inspiring resistance to Christianity. As Christianity gained more followers and power, pagan rituals were systematically stamped out. The former sites of great pagan ritual and learning were destroyed or turned into churches throughout the 4th and 5th centuries CE. The temple of Demeter was sacked leaving only ruins, where once the people of the ancient world gathered to experience the truths of life, death and rebirth.[13]

# Priestesses of Artemis

The Temple of Artemis was an ancient Greek temple dedicated to the goddess Artemis,[14] located in the ancient city of Ephesus, near present-day Selçuk in Turkey.[15] There were also many other temples throughout Greece devoted to Artemis, such was her impact on the Greek people. Artemis was the Greek goddess of hunting, wild animals, forests, young women, childbirth, fertility and chastity.[16]

Artemis's main temple was noted for its wealth and splendour which spoke to her power and prestige as a goddess.[17] Large numbers of people came to the temple in March and May every year to attend the Artemis Procession where games, contests and theatrical performances were held in her name.

Artemis's temple was tended to by holy women under the direction of a priestess who came to her role via inheritance. Standards for Artemis priestesses were very strict in relation to sexual purity and they had to remain virgins throughout their service.

Thanks to the worship of and belief in Artemis, large sections of the Greek landscape were preserved for many years. For this reason,

Artemis and her devoted priestesses were seen as early patronesses of environmental education and are responsible for many of the conservation efforts of Classical Greece.[18]

# The Melissai

In ancient Greece, in the goddess temples of Artemis, Aphrodite, Demeter, Cybele, Diana and Rhea, priestesses were called *melissai* or 'the bees'. 'Melissa' was a title of honour, bestowed only upon those most devoted to the Great Mother.

To the ancient Greeks the bee was not only a messenger but a direct representative of the gods and goddesses.[19] The ability of bees to create honey was believed to be magical and divine, and because bees were never seen to engage in sex, they were also seen as powerful symbols of virginity. Being a virgin was central to the life of a Melissa, as was being spiritually diligent. A Melissa's devotion to her goddess often involved eating a toxic honey as a psychotropic drug to heighten her spiritual perceptions and divine connection.

Melissai were honoured in ancient Greek society due to their knowing of how to live peacefully with the laws of nature and maintaining a balance with the land around them. As priestesses and devotees of the goddess, they represented healing, strength, divine inspiration and creative power.

# Priestesses of Athena

The priestesses of Athena Polias at Athens were deemed so important in ancient Greek civilisation that events were dated according to their names. In honour of their commitment to Athena, the patron goddess of Athens, war and wisdom, they were often paid and given property, and they were much respected for their contributions to society. Ancient Greek priestesses were held in such popular regard that they could even be seen as the celebrities of their time.

High priestess of Athena was the most important religious position in Athens, and she was always a woman from an Eteoboutadae noble family.

The Panathenaia festival was held every year to honour Athena's birthday and every fourth year, the Greater Panathenaia was held, which included a grand procession to the Acropolis. In preparation for the procession, a new robe was made for the statue of Athena at the Acropolis. Two girls from noble families were chosen to live with the priestesses of Athena leading up to the procession so that they could assist in the weaving of the garment for the goddess.

# The Pythia

---

The Pythia was the high priestess and oracle of the Temple of Apollo at Delphi. The Pythia was widely credited for her prophecies inspired by the god Apollo from the 7th century BCE until the 4th century CE. During this period of time, the Pythia was seen to be the most powerful woman of the classical world, and authors who mention her include Aristotle, Plato and Sophocles.

The Pythia were all natives of Delphi, and although some were married, upon assuming the role as the Pythia, they ceased all family responsibilities, marriage and personal identity. The Pythia was sometimes from an influential family and well educated, but in later periods uneducated peasant women were chosen for the role, suggesting it was aptitude rather than status that made them eligible to speak for Apollo.

Any person seeking the counsel of the Pythia would offer her laurel branches, money and sometimes a black ram. To allow Apollo to speak through her the Pythia would bathe in the Castalian Spring and then descend into a special chamber beneath the temple which was fumigated with barley meal and laurel leaves. Sitting on a covered tripod cauldron enveloped by vapours, the Pythia would fall into a trance and channel Apollo.[20]

The job of a priestess, especially the Pythia, was a respectable career for Greek women. Priestesses enjoyed many liberties such as having the right to own property, not pay taxes, attend public events and be provided housing by the state. All Pythias were especially known to have powerful tools of divination and dream interpretation.

# The Vestal Priestesses

The Vestal priestesses, also known as the Vestal Virgins, served the goddess of hearth and home, Vesta, in ancient Rome. They were the only full-time servants of a Roman deity and tended the sacred fire in the shrine of Vesta housed in the Roman Forum. Here, they also cared for the shrine's sacred objects, prepared ritual food and herbs, and officiated at public events.

Between four and six priestesses were employed at any one time to serve Vesta. They were required to be virgins throughout their thirty years of service. They were chosen for the role at between six and ten years of age, and their physical strength and morality and the stature of their parents were all taken into consideration before they were selected. Male clergy were not allowed to participate in any rites concerning the Vestal priestesses.

Once their service was completed, Vestal priestesses were free to marry, but very few chose to do so as they were considered to be the brides of Vesta and were tied to her forever. Marriage as a Roman woman would also mean total submission to their husband's authority and this likely would have been a suffocating thought for a Vestal priestess who had been given many privileges usually reserved for upper class Roman men including being able to vote.

If a Vestal priestess failed in her duties she was severely beaten, and if she lost her virginity or let the temple fire go out, she was executed, often by being buried alive. It was a very strong incentive for her to remain chaste and work hard. Vestal priestesses had all of their needs provided for by the temple and were free of the restrictions other Roman women had to endure. It was because they were so highly regarded that the punishment of breaking their vows was made so severe.

The Vestal priestesses were a significant part of Roman life until 394 CE when the Christian emperor Theodosius I issued a decree against pagan rituals and had Vesta's sacred fire put out.

## Celtic Priestesses

In ancient Celtic society, priestesses were a part of an intellectual elite focused on the Mother Goddess and earth-based beliefs of the religion that was later to be known as Druidism.[21] Their training was extensive and included learnings in literature, poetry, history, law and astronomy. Female Celtic spiritual leaders were known as druidesses (male counterparts druids) and seers, as well as priestesses.

Celtic priestesses mediated for their communities, performed sacrifices, interpreted omens, taught young men the survival arts of hunting and fishing, and presided over religious ceremonies to support people to connect with Celtic goddesses and gods.[22] They also often advised royalty who looked to their dreams and prophecies to interpret and predict events, especially in relation to politics and conflict.

Some Celtic priestesses lived a more isolated life than a community-based one and lived on offshore islands. In the first century BCE a group of Celtic priestesses lived on an island near the mouth of the River Loire where they worshipped an unknown goddess, and the priestesses of the island of Sena were said to be able to predict the future, cure disease and control the weather.[23]

From the first century CE Roman invaders began to restrain priestesses, and Celtic society slowly changed from one centred around the honouring of a Mother Goddess and viewing women as equal to men, to one upholding a view of them chiefly as childbearers and pleasure objects. By the Middle Ages women were pushed out of their roles as spiritual leaders and diminished to the roles of nun and abbess. Women's high status in the Celtic world was wiped out.

After the downfall of traditional Druidism, Christianity became the main religion on the British Isles and former priestesses were relegated to witch-like figures, synonymous with the work of the devil. Christians feared the priestesses due to their religious power and being a source of spiritual knowledge, connection and counsel for their people.

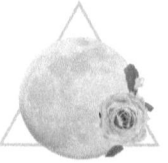

# Völur

Völur were seeresses of Seidr, a form of magic and shamanism during the Viking Age of 800 to 1050 CE.[24]

The völur carried out *Seidr*, also known as Seid, using a wand, songs and a special seat which they believed enabled the soul to travel. The völva would sit on the seat holding her wand, and the song she would sing, or was sung to her by young girls, would send her into a trance where she visited spirits and gods. She would state her purpose to them and in this place between two worlds she could answer questions about someone's future and fate. Seidr rituals were also undertaken by völur to form prophecies, blessings or curses.[25] [26]

Female graves of wealthy women from the Viking era have been found containing items such as wands, cauldrons, cannabis, carriages, bronze jugs and silver jewellery, emphasising the fact that the völur belonged to the upper classes and were deeply respected. Some völur were even buried in ships which also contained sacrificed animals and humans.[27]

With the onset of Christianity, the völur stopped practising Seidr and by the Middle Ages, the Danish word for seeress meant witch, and their rituals were seen to be harmful. Laws were issued to suppress Seidr and all magic was forbidden.[28]

The Norse goddess Freyja is the archetype of the völur and it was she who was believed by them to bring forth the art and magic of Seidr.[29]

## Mayan Priestesses

The Mayan people (1800 BCE to 900 CE) of Mesoamerica—a cultural and historical region of the Americas incorporating today central Mexico, Belize, Guatemala, El Salvador, Honduras, Nicaragua and northern Costa Rica—worshipped a rich pantheon of goddesses and gods in which women played important spiritual roles.[30]

Women have been depicted in ancient Mayan art performing priestess rituals honouring the calendar year as well as important astronomical events such as the lunar cycles and eclipses. They also conducted ceremonies honouring the goddesses and gods which included songs, prayers and incense, as well as sacrificial bloodletting offerings. Mayan priestesses also led pilgrimages to sacred sites that were most often dedicated to the goddess Ix Chel, the goddess of fertility, midwifery, medicine and weaving. The priestesses would guide pilgrims along trails to these sites and serve as diviners and fortune tellers as well.[31]

Women also held powerful spiritual and practical roles in Mayan culture as midwives.[32] This important and prestigious role was believed to be spiritually assigned to them through dreams and visions. They held no formal training to be a midwife but were known to communicate with the supernatural world for the betterment of pregnant and birthing women and their babies. They received all they needed to fulfil the role from being called to it.

By 900 CE, much of Mayan civilisation had declined and this was further compounded by Spanish colonisation of Mesoamerica in the 1500s, which saw millions of indigenous people killed, entire villages relocated and given new Christian names, and churches replaced sacred sites. Women lost much of their social, economic and religious power through patriarchal and religious oppression. Despite this, many Mayan beliefs and practices, especially those connected to fertility and female sexuality, were never fully eradicated, and women throughout South America today continue to play important roles in the spiritual wellbeing of their communities.

# Moche Priestesses

The Moche culture and religion was practised by the people of northern Peru from 100 to 800 CE. The Moche worshipped many deities, the most powerful of whom was the moon goddess Si.

Until very recently scholars believed that only men held important roles in Moche religion. However, with the discovery of priestess burial tombs and learning that Moche history was largely depicted on ceramics, which has widely shown women performing important rituals, this has become unfounded.[33] [34]

The Moche priestess tombs found in 1991 show the important role women played in their religion. Objects found in the elaborate and multi-roomed tombs include necklaces, fine ceramics and large plumed priestess headdresses, as well as goblets that were used to collect the blood of human sacrifices in ritual ceremonies.[35] Other human remains were also found buried with the priestesses, indicating that numerous people were sacrificed at a priestess's death as an offering to the goddesses and gods. Human sacrifice was a common part of the Moche[36] religion.[37]

Moche priestesses also held political roles similar to that of a governor, and were also seen as having oracular powers and revered for their wise counsel.

# Mambos

Mambos are female initiates and priestesses of the Haitian religion Vodou.[38] The word mambo means 'mother of the spirit.'[39]

Followers of Vodou believe that the law of God should be followed by being in constant communion with spirit beings and one's ancestors. Spirits are praised in ceremony to ward off evil and impact destiny positively. In Vodou, spirit refers to both revered ancestor spirits as well as spirit forces or deities called loa, also written *lwa*, who followers believe can be found everywhere.

Through initiation a mambo is aligned with the spirit world to receive guidance to support others with their own spiritual connections. Through these messages as well as prayer and ritual, she guides Vodou followers to a deeper and richer spiritual life. Mambos do not preach, but rather serve to help in the spiritual growth of others and protect their communities.

There are two ranks of mambo in Vodou: *su pwen* and *asogwe*. A mambo su pwen shadows and assists a mambo asogwe so they can learn how to perform ceremonies and rituals and facilitate healing for people. Mambos are also taught skills in divination and dream interpretation. A mambo asogwe demonstrates great spiritual knowledge and selfless service and is known to be a facilitator of the Divine. They may be called upon to support their local community with various roles including birth and death ceremonies, marriage mediation and grief counselling. A mambo asogwe's time is largely charitably devoted to her community, where she is charged with bringing peace and prosperity to those around her.

## Santeras

Santeras are priestesses of the syncretic Afro-Cuban religion Santería, which chiefly originated in Cuba. Followers of Santería worship Yoruban gods and goddesses, known as Orishas, with a blended acknowledgement of Catholic saints.[40] Santería is also known as Regla de Ocha or lucumí.

Santería has its roots in the Yoruba people of West Africa. Kidnapped and forced into slavery during the transatlantic slave trade of 1600 to 1900 CE, millions of African people were shipped to countries such as Cuba, Brazil, Haiti, Puerto Rico, Trinidad, the USA and the Caribbean, where they were not allowed to openly practise their religions. Most often forced to convert to Catholicism, the enslaved African people syncretised their Orishas with Catholic saints to ensure the pretence of keeping up Christian appearances for their enslavers.[41]

Unlike the Catholic church, where women's roles are and have always been very limited, Santería honours women as priestesses due to the very central role they played in all aspects of Yoruba culture.[42] To be initiated as a santera involves undergoing a series of initiations and ceremonies that require complete spiritual devotion.[43] These rituals guide the santera through a process where she is cleansed and reborn into a deep spiritual path and life with her Orisha as her guide.[44]

Santeras are revered for being herbalists and use flowers and herbs extensively in their offerings and practices, which are rich in ceremony and ritual. Practising chiefly from a house temple, santeras are called upon by their community to provide herbalism-based healthcare, divination and spiritual guidance from and in alignment with the Orishas. Santeras also serve their Orishas through animal sacrifice offerings, altar craft and extensive use of music and dance practices.[45]

# PART III

*Power Priestesses*

If you have been wondering if we know anything of real-life priestesses, I am so delighted to share with you that we do.

The women in power priestesses held incredible roles throughout history as spiritual leaders, healers and warriors. Some were gently devoted to the Goddess—and sometimes gods—and their calling in honour of her name. Others were fierce and unrelenting in their search for justice and liberation for their people, impacting the lives of untold numbers to alleviate poverty, hunger and the traumatic impacts of colonisation and white supremacy. They were in devoted service from grand temples and palaces, on the back of horses, on battlefields and in houses of their local communities.

The priestesses I share with you will not be only the ones known to us.

For every one of these women in historically recorded roles, there will be untold numbers who served their goddesses and communities whose names we will never know. Their contribution to the ancestral DNA we all carry is just as vital as that of any lineage that may have found its way into the pages of *Priestess*.

# Enheduanna

---

Enheduanna was a poet and priestess from Sumer and is the world's first named author. She was the daughter of King Sargon of Agade and the high priestess of the most important temple in ancient Sumer, in what is today southern Iraq.[1]

Enheduanna is credited with creating the structure of poetry, psalms and prayers we still widely use today. She is best known for her hymns to the goddess Inanna, and was responsible for the religious health and wellbeing of the people of Sumer. Her work drew the gods and goddesses closer to people in everyday life.

Enheduanna's role as a priestess involved the upkeep and restoration of Inanna's temple, known as a *giparu*, the performing of water rites, composing hymns of praise and carrying offerings in a ritual basket which was used to bring grains, honey and dates as a fertility offering. Enheduanna was also a political mediator mirroring her father's authority with the military, where she was seen to represent the union of the divine and civil, religion and state, gods and kings.

A calcite disc belonging to Enheduanna was excavated in 1927 with the inscription:

> Enheduanna, zirru-priestess, wife of the god Nanna, daughter of Sargon, king of the world, in the temple of the goddess Inanna.

Her own figure was placed prominently on the disc, emphasising Enheduanna's supreme importance and influence on the culture of her time.

# Ennigaldi-Nanna

Ennigaldi-Nanna, also known as Bel-Shalti-Nannar and Princess Ennigaldi, lived in the sixth century BCE in Babylonia, an ancient Akkadian-speaking state of central-southern Mesopotamia, in what is today known as Iraq. Ennigaldi-Nanna was the daughter of the last king of Ur, Nabonidus, who reigned in an ancient city located today in Tell el-Muqayyar.[2]

Ennigaldi-Nanna was a high priestess, also known as an entu-priestess of the moon god Nanna, and she undertook her priestess rituals and devotion in a small sacred room called a *giparu* in the Great Ziggurat of Ur, a temple built in Nanna's honour. No men were permitted to enter this sacred room.

Supported by her father in 530 BCE, Ennigaldi-Nanna established a museum focused on the cultural history of Mesopotamia where she was both its curator and researcher. The museum was active until around 500 BCE when Ur had to be abandoned due to prolonged drought. The museum was excavated by an archaeologist in 1925, where the museum's contents were found to be categorised and labelled using clay tablets and drums.

It is thought that Ennigaldi-Nanna may have led a priestess training school in the Great Ziggurat, but no formal evidence of this has been found.

# Hatshepsut

Hatshepsut (1479 to 1458 BCE) was one of the most prominent female rulers of ancient Egypt. She was the daughter of Thutmose I and Queen Ahmose and was granted the priestess position of God's Wife of Amun before she was twenty years old. In this role Hatshepsut presided over festivals honouring the god Amun, giving her more power than a queen.

Hatshepsut became the regent of Egypt when her husband died. Her stepson, Thutmose III, was a child and unable to assume the pharaoh role at the time, and so Hatshepsut took care of state affairs on his behalf. In her seventh year of regency, Hatshepsut crowned herself pharaoh. While she took on all royal titles and names in inscriptions using the feminine grammatical form, she chose to have herself depicted as a male pharaoh on statues and in artefacts. Why this is so is not fully known. It may have been that she believed this would assist her in being taken seriously in the role of pharaoh, or that she may have considered herself to be gender fluid and both woman and man as a supreme ruler.

Hatshepsut put numerous things in place to strengthen her rule as pharaoh including elevating her daughter to be a God's Wife of Amun, presenting herself not only as Amun's wife but as his daughter, making her a demi-goddess, and claiming she was a direct successor to her father. This was to defend against detractors who might claim a woman was unfit to rule as pharaoh.

Hatshepsut commissioned many building projects during her prosperous reign that were built on a grander scale and employed more people than those of any pharaoh before her. Very few museums featuring ancient Egyptian artefacts today do not have some piece commissioned by her.

When Thutmose III eventually took rule as pharaoh, he back dated his reign to the death of his father and Hatshepsut's accomplishments were ascribed to him, erasing all evidence of her rule. However, once Hatshepsut's name was found—in the inner chambers of a temple she had built for herself—in the nineteenth century CE, she assumed her rightful place as one of the greatest pharaohs in Egyptian history. Modern-day archaeological testing found that Hatshepsut died in her fifties from a tooth abscess.

# Onomaris

---

Onomaris was a Celtic priestess and leader from Gaul, which today covers numerous countries throughout Western Europe.[3] Her name means mountain ash or rowan tree, which are sacred trees to the Celtic people, considered to have magical and healing properties.

In their written history in the late 300s BCE, the Greeks wrote of a Celtic tribe who were led by Onomaris to settle along the banks of the Danube River at Singidunum in Serbia, what is known today as Belgrade.[4] Onomaris led her people there due to the tribes' failing crops, which saw their children malnourished and dying.

No men in the Celtic tribe stepped forth in leadership to find a solution for their lack of food and so Onomaris did so herself,[5] pooling all property of the tribe and dividing it up equally among families before making the long trip across harsh terrain.[6] Onomaris encountered regular battles with enemies along the way.[7] It is said she used her powers of prophecy to know that the region of the Danube was the right place to lead the tribe.

Upon arrival and settlement, Onomaris ruled the new territory as queen and her courage and leadership were noted by the Greeks in showing them that Celtic women, unlike women in general in their own society, could hold great spiritual and leadership power.

# Chrysis

Chrysis was a priestess of Athena Polias in ancient Greece.

As a priestess, Chrysis was considered to be a special representative of Athens and did not pay taxes, had front row seats at all city-held competitions and could own land. Chrysis's great-great-grandfather was a sacred supervisor of the Eleusinian Mysteries and her grandfather a priest of Asklepios. Chrysis was considered to be an outstanding woman and a statue of her could be found at the Athenian Acropolis during her time in service.[8]

Chrysis served as an honoured priestess for fifty years until in 423 BCE, after placing a candle near a curtain, she accidentally burned down the temple of Argos. She survived the fire but fled Argos to the nearby city of Phlius. Pausanias believes she then reached Tegea, where she found refuge at the sanctuary of Athena Alea.[9] The fire at Argos was later deliberately misconstrued by Christian theologians, some of whom said she did die in the fire as an example of the impotence of the heathen gods.

# Boudicca

Boudicca (about 30 to 61 CE) was a Celtic queen and priestess of the Iceni tribe which occupied modern-day East Anglia in Britain.[10] She was devoted to the Celtic goddess of war and victory Andraste.[11]

After Boudicca's husband died, his estate was inherited equally by his two daughters and King Nero of Rome to maintain the Iceni's tentative alliance with British-occupying Romans. Boudicca took over the reign of the Iceni upon his death, but her husband's bequest of land to his daughters was not recognised by the Romans and they claimed it for themselves.

When Boudicca objected to this, she was publicly flogged, and both her daughters were raped. Enraged, Boudicca called upon the Iceni to rise up in revenge, mounting a revolt which left over 80,000 Romans occupying Britain dead.[12] Known to be an unflinching and relentless warrior, Boudicca never took prisoners, and killed both women and men by brutal means. The Romans reported her to be fiercely tall and strong with a wild mass of red hair.[13]

As a priestess of Andraste, Boudicca prayed to the goddess to support her and the Iceni in battle, and used the art of divination—often with a hare which she saw as her sacred animal—to predict the right direction for her warriors to go into combat.

The exact details of Boudicca's death are not known; however, it is widely believed she killed herself by taking poison in an effort to evade capture soon after her final defeat in battle. Boudicca was given a lavish burial by her people and remains celebrated today as a heroine who fought for freedom and justice.

A statue of Boudicca and her daughters was erected in 1902 in London.

# Veleda

Veleda was a priestess, prophet and seer of the Bructeri tribe of Germany. Her name in the Teutonic (Germanic) language means 'inspired intelligence'. Veleda was revered as a great deity and as an unmarried woman she possessed widespread political and diplomatic authority.[14]

In 69 to 70 CE Veleda predicted the Bructeri's initial success against Roman rebels and helped guide their battle strategy in conjunction with tribe chieftains. She reached a great height of fame for her work which she undertook in a tower near the Lippe River, a tributary of the Rhine. The virgin Veleda was said to perform her divination in complete seclusion, charging one of her relatives with the responsibility to deliver the information she gleaned.

The people of ancient Germany regarded the skill of prophecy highly not just in Veleda, but in any woman who displayed oracular skills. Rather than being regarded with suspicion or mistrust, women's divination skills were seen to enormously enhance the lives of all those around them, especially in matters of state and warfare.

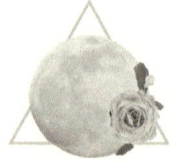

# Fidelm

Fidelm was a *banfhili* (priestess) and *banfhaith* (woman prophet) from Connacht, Ireland, who is reported to have lived during the tenth century CE. Fidelm received esoteric training in Alba, modern-day Scotland, to heighten her prophecy skills, and was known for her great beauty and long hair.[15]

Fidelm served as a banfhili in the court of Queen Medb of Connacht and, like her Bructeri counterpart Veleda, had a similar prophetess role in predicting the outcome of battles. Unlike the virgin Veleda, Fidelm was said to be a sexually powerful woman and the lover of the young Irish hero, Cú Chulainn. Fidelm is mentioned in the *Táin Bó Cúailnge* (The Cattle Raid of Cooley), an epic Irish tale, in which she is questioned by Queen Medb about the fate of one of her armies and her meeting with Cú Chulainn.[16]

Like Cú Chulainn himself, it is not certain if Fidelm was a mythical character or walked the earth. Hundreds of years of retelling of tales, stories, myths and legends make her humanness not fully known. Despite this, whether as woman or mythical character, Fidelm's skills of prophecy as a priestess highlight the importance of such skills in women in Celtic society.

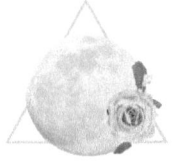

# Mary Magdalene

Mary Magdalene was a Jewish woman who travelled with Jesus of Nazareth as one of his followers and disciples.[17]

Mary came from the town of Magdala, an ancient city in Israel, and all four canonical gospels written in the first century CE, considered to be the most important texts of the Christian religion, mention her. The gospels indicate Mary was a vital part of Jesus's ministry and that she was witness to his crucifixion and burial.[18] In the Gospel of John, Jesus portrays Mary as his most important apostle, Christian teacher, when he sends her to the other male apostles to announce his resurrection.[19]

By the Middle Ages, Mary was widely presented as a sinful prostitute, particularly by the Roman Catholic Church, but there is no evidence to support this or that she was anything but a devoted follower of Christ. In 1969, the identification of Mary in this way was removed from the General Roman Calendar, an admission by the church that their portrayal of her in this way was false.

From the High Middle Ages many writers and artists began developing fictional biographies about Mary which embellished tales of her wealth, social status and sexuality, and the exact details of the final part of her life are not known. It is widely accepted that Mary was a real person, and she is now revered as a saint by a variety of churches.

While many may not view Mary as a priestess, given that she was such a prominent part of the religion that played a large role in the oppression of goddess culture, her undeniable service to people through her religious devotion can easily see her noted in this way. Patriarchal and dogmatic religious forces tried to reduce Mary's humility and service to others in a way that was designed to serve as an oppressive warning to all women to not follow suit. However, Mary's love and the power of her devotion have managed to survive hundreds of years of patriarchal oppression, to now see her honoured as the true spiritual leader and priestess she was.

# Queen Himiko

Queen Himiko of Yamatai, an ancient country in Wa (a former name for what is today Japan), lived during the Yavoi period of about 300 BCE to 300 CE, and is the first named (male or female) figure in Japanese history. She was a shamaness beloved for her peaceful rule and diplomatic savvy. Chosen by her people in 190 CE as an unmarried priestess to rule them, Himiko reigned peacefully for more than half a decade.

Himiko's name in ancient Japanese mentions 'sun child' or 'sun daughter', alluding to her being seen as a divine offspring of the Shinto sun goddess Amaterasu. Himiko was widely known to be able to speak to gods and goddesses, and female shamans were highly regarded in Yamatai during her reign. She lived in a palace and was served by 1000 priestesses. It is said she was a recluse and never married.

Himiko died in 248 CE. She is widely beloved in Japan today despite years of patriarchy attempting to suppress the details of her reign. She symbolises female occult power and is particularly beloved by children.

Scholars today still debate who Himiko exactly was and how much of the country of Japan she may have ruled, including the potential she oversaw all of it. She has a fabled burial mound, but there is no consensus on where it is located.

# Aconia Fabia Paulina

Aconia Fabia Paulina (died about 384 CE) was one of the last pagan Romans who tried to save the Roman religion from decline before the onset of Christianity. She was the daughter of a prominent aristocrat, and her husband, also a member of the aristocracy, was an imperial officer and member of several pagan circles.[20]

Aconia Fabia Paulina was initiated into the Eleusinian mysteries which honoured the goddess Demeter and her daughter Persephone.[21] Initially based at Eleusis in ancient Greece, the mysteries later spread to Rome. The mysteries represented the myth of the abduction of Persephone from Demeter by the king of the underworld Hades, in a cycle with three phases: the descent, the search and the ascent with the eventual reunion of mother and daughter. For the initiated, the rebirth of Persephone symbolised the eternity of life which flowed from generation to generation.

Aconia Fabia was also known to be devoted to several other goddesses including Ceres, Hecate, Cybele and Isis.

# Brigid

Brigid was born in Faughart, Ireland, about 453 to 524 CE and was a Celtic ban-druí or druidess.[22] Brigid (or Bridget) founded many orders with Celtic traditions and both men and women were abundant in the communities she presided over religiously. Brigid contributed her Celtic beliefs to a changing world throughout Great Britain, and in particular, she promoted equality among women and men.[23] Her conversion to Christianity contributed significantly to the fall of Druidism and the Celtic religion, a testament to how widely she was followed and loved.[24]

The cult of Brigid was kept alive through her naming as a Christian saint, which connected her memory with the Celtic goddess Brighde. Brighde represented warmth, fire and summer and she was celebrated with a shrine in Kildare County where a sacred flame burned, tended by a number of priestesses.[25] The flame burned continuously until 1220 CE through its transition into a Christian nunnery when Archbishop Henry of Dublin ordered it to be extinguished. At the time of the shrine's conversion into a nunnery, the Christian order dedicated it solely to the woman known as St Brigid instead of the goddess whose memory they wanted to disappear.[26]

Much of Brigid's life is mixed with myth and legend. She is loved and revered not just throughout Ireland but in many countries throughout the world, resulting in her being claimed by many individuals and groups in the way they choose to see her. This means she is sometimes depicted as a druidess, a nun, a saint, a goddess and more. Her legend and influence transcend time.

# Dahia al-Kahina

Dahia al-Kahina was a Moor prophetess, soothsayer and warrior from Tunisia.[27] She is also known as Dihya and the *kahina*, which means 'seer' in Arabic. She was the leader of a Judaised Berber tribe from Algeria.[28] Dahia led the Berber resistance in the seventh century CE, with initial success in North Africa against an invading Arab army.[29] A few years later when the Arabian army invaded again, Dahia was pursued into the mountains where she was killed in combat.[30] A well that she died near has been named in her memory.

The exact facts surrounding Dahia's life and death are not fully known. Since the ninth century she has been revered and claimed by a variety of social, political and cultural groups including those of Arabic, Berber, Muslim and Jewish background. Statues honouring Dahia have been erected in Algeria and in the town of Baghaï where a fortress was discovered that many people believe she erected to oppose the advancing Arab army.[31]

Whether Dahia actually existed remains unknown, but her courage and resistance have inspired millions of people aspiring to religious and ethnic tolerance. Her work therefore, as a real or mythic priestess, lives on.

# Marie Laveau

Marie Laveau (1801 to 1881) was a Vodou priestess from New Orleans, and such was her prominence and notoriety that at the height of her power, some say she was the real political and social leader of the city.[32] Born free, Marie was of African, Native American and French descent. Marie was also Catholic, and her influence contributed significantly to the adoption of Catholic practices into Vodou.[33]

As a Vodou priestess, Marie led ceremonial meetings and ritual dances which sometimes drew crowds of thousands.[34] Her spiritual power was recognised by politicians, judges, criminals and slaves, and it was said that many prominent men consulted her before making any important decision relating to their finances or business. Marie was a compassionate champion for her people, especially slaves, and very public in her resistance to white supremacist oppression.

Marie was not a conventionally passive and modest woman, usual of her time. Rather she was a bold and assertive black spiritual leader, and while her life has been surrounded by legend, she had an undeniably real influence on the people and city of New Orleans.

Marie died of natural causes, and an obituary in the *New York Times* stated that a great number of prominent New Orleans citizens came to pay their respects to her. Her grave site is still a major tourist attraction with many visitors offering gifts and praying to her spirit there.

# Nehanda Charwe Nyakasikana

Nehanda Charwe Nyakasikana (1862? to 1898) was a *svikiro* (spirit medium) and *mhondoro* (royal ancestral spirit) in both Zimbabwean and South African culture.[35] Her legacy transcends national boundaries throughout Africa.

At birth Nehanda Nyakasikana was considered to be the female incarnation of the great oracle Nehanda, who is commonly referred to as the grandmother of present-day Zimbabwe and an early resistor to European colonialism.[36] The African resistance in the 1800s was known as the Chimurenga War and was led and supported by three traditional spiritual leaders of which Nehanda was the only woman.

In 1897, Nehanda was captured at the war's end and charged with the murder of a local commissioner, which is widely acknowledged now to have been a false charge. Despite this, Nehanda was found guilty and hanged by the British High Commissioner in 1898.[37] Her dying words were, *'Mapfupa angu achamuka!'* ('My bones will surely rise!').[38] Throughout all of her encounters with British invaders, the colonial government and missionaries, Nehanda refused to convert to Christianity.

When the nationalist liberation movements of the 1960s and 1970s rose in Africa, Zimbabwe's local guerrilla factions conducted ceremonies to raise the spirit of Nehanda in their independence struggle.

# Fermina Gómez Pastrana

Fermina Gómez Pastrana (1844 to 1950) was one of the best-known and respected priestesses of the Santería religion in Cuba.[39]

Fermina was born Maria Pilar Gómez Pastrana, in the province of Matanzas, Cuba. She was initially initiated to the Orisha (a deity or multi-dimensional unity that links people, power and objects of the Yoruba people of southwest Africa) Ochún, by a priest, even though she was considered to be a daughter of the Orisha Yemayá. Within her first year of initiation Fermina experienced a psychological and spiritual breakdown which saw her seek help from the Priestess Ma Monserrate Gonzalez, also known as Oba Tero. Oba Tero 'corrected' Fermina's initial initiation to the wrong Orisha and named her Ocha Bi.[40]

Fermina was widely known to be a transformative priestess and performed many rare and complex initiations.[41] According to elders of Santería, she was particularly devoted to supporting members of her black community to reframe racial trauma. She created rituals which brought together the Orishas, ancestral spirits and dead slave-warriors into a person's body so they could heal. For these rituals, Fermina particularly called upon the Orisha Olókun, who is believed to govern the depths of the ocean.[42] Fermina felt Olókun was key to soothing the turmoil of slaves and in 1944 she began a tradition of 'feeding' Olókun at the ocean to give back to those slaves who died at sea being transported from Africa to Cuba.[43]

Fermina lived to be 107 years old.

# PART IV

# The Inner Calling and Being

In this current day of pretty Instagram photos, visually sumptuous Pinterest pins and culturally appropriated spiritual knick-knacks, it's easy to believe that being a priestess is something that can be readily shown and known.

**However, the path of the priestess is an inner calling and being. First, foremost and always.**

How that calling may show itself to you and then be shown by you to the wider world is different for everyone. What is certain is that it's not just about what you do, the sacred circles you may hold or the healing you may offer. And it's certainly not about the size of your altar, or how much time you spend in meditation every day.

**It cannot be just the word 'priestess' that attracts you. That is not being called.**

To be truly called is to have a feeling of longing from deep inside you It is a soul whisper, that often crescendos into a roar, that not only is something right for you, it is something that must be accepted and followed and become an intrinsic part of who you are.

**That is being called.**

The inner calling, and being, is designed to help you begin or deepen your relationship with your spiritual self as someone who is hearing the calling that a part of your life is meant to be unveiled and lived as a spiritual leader and priestess. It is a whisper, voice or roar that is calling you within. Each small section is designed to get you feeling, thinking and being into a deep understanding that if you desire to be a spiritual leader you must firstly, foremostly, and always work on your own self. That you cannot bypass the work necessary to your own healing and to know that as you do, you step onto a lifelong path of commitment.

There are goddesses noted in each section that are particularly powerful and relevant to each step of this work. You may like to call upon them in support, exploration and adventure to be with you as you journey. I encourage you in doing so to choose goddesses to actively explore and work with that are culturally relevant and appropriate to you.

There are so many goddesses across cultures that represent core themes of creativity, love, compassion, health, darkness, fertility and more. If you work with those, once upon a time your ancestors likely will have as well, the riches that will unfold for you in doing so will be so much greater than selecting goddesses to work with that simply seem to be a popular choice of the moment. You will find something inside yourself that is at once rooted in the land of your ancestors and ethereally divine as you connect deeper to your highest self.

**Let's go within ...**

# Guide Me, Goddess

Consciously choosing to work with a goddess can truly enhance your work and being as a priestess and spiritual leader. It can also support you in your everyday life in infinite ways that you may not know you need; but She will show you if you open to Her.

Ancient priestesses were often devoted to one particular goddess or god. And of course, these were deities from their own culture and land. And it's always going to be most powerful for you to choose to call in and work with goddesses from your own lineage and culture too, as you open this part of yourself.

When you work with and call upon the goddess as a guide, know in essence that you are calling on yourself. She exists to help you connect with a human figure of love and power so that you may see yourself in Her. She takes a human form—sometimes with added special wings, tails, feathers!—so that you can visually relate to Her and connect with Her presence. And what She can do for you as an ally is infinite, supporting and inspiring you with your spiritual work, especially the work you are called to do within.

Goddesses themes are designed to help bring you into a greater wholeness and centredness, one where you feel more balanced in both your light and shadow. Those themes may be related to love, creativity, health, relationships, fear, transformation, your inner child, relationships and so much more. You may already know some goddesses and be particularly intrigued by them, as there are thousands of them, and likely more. There are also going to be many that you may never have heard of but could still come to you if your relationship is meant to be.

What the goddess will tell you will only ever be what you need. You may think you hear a lie in what She says or that something She has is not right for you. It is. She is a companion and a true friend. She will tell you only your highest and most needed truth. If you want to work with a goddess, then you must be prepared to surrender and trust in that process and in Her wholeheartedly. You must trust *yourself* wholeheartedly. You cannot take up the call to be a priestess or even simply work with the goddess deeply if you're not prepared to hear it all. The good. The bad. The in between. The call to do better. Back yourself into being with Her and know you can handle it.

The ways in which you can connect to a goddess are limited only by your imagination and what you are open to seeing and experiencing around you. You may:

- ☆ see signs of Her appear to you in nature, your thoughts, books, art, or music, calling you to make a connection with Her.
- ☆ work with an oracle card deck where She repeatedly comes to you through divination or even just once in a blinding flash of presence.
- ☆ curiously research a particular goddess, goddesses or archetypes to match your stage of life or current needs and then consciously call Her to support you. She may then come, or send a proxy that is even more of what you need.

- ☆ see and feel Her come to you in your dreams either one time or many.
- ☆ see Her, or themes and signs of Her when you are in stillness, prayer, meditation or silence.
- ☆ consciously call for Her to come to you for your highest good in meditation.

And when She does come to you, with whatever loving lessons and insights She is supposed to deliver, it is then in your hands as to how deeply you choose to be with Her. You may choose to talk with Her every day in your meditations or prayers to see what She continues to share with you. You can devote a part of or even your entire altar space to Her so that She knows She is welcome near you at any time. Cooking with or eating foods you know that She loves or are important to Her can make you feel closer to each other, as can wearing Her known colours, connecting with Her particular moon or sun phases and using herbs, plants and oils that are powerful to Her stories, presence and gifts.

A guiding goddess will remain with you for a moment, a day, a month, or years depending upon what She has to share with you. As you grow and deepen into Her lessons for you, She may become stronger and more intent in what She has to share. She may also, as you now know happened to me, become softer and fade into the background of your higher counsel, to make way for the next chapter of your spiritual journey. This may be something you want and embrace. Or it may not be. Either way know that She knows best for you.

**Because you know best for you.**

---

*Goddesses:*
*All*

---

# The Great Work

Your best *work* in life is always going to be done as an inside job. Capitalism, patriarchy and their sidekicks like the media, just to name one of their oppressive players, would love to convince you that the most important part of your life is what you look like. How much money you earn. How many likes you're getting on social media, and the status of your friends.

It's a ruse.

It's a ruse designed to keep us small, eternally spending money and focused on comparing ourselves to each other.

However, the most revelatory and life-changing work we can do as a person is that which calls us in. To that place or places where we tell ourselves we're not as good as someone else. Where our jealousy, pride and lies live. Where we feel and keep ourselves separate. Where shame has its own little postcode.

And also to those places where we truly know we shine. Where our skills and passions collide and we desire to be seen as someone magnificent and beautiful, even if it makes us feel uncomfortable or afraid. To where we know if we can move beyond our imposter complex to a place of heartfelt acceptance, we could truly step out into the world and be seen. No pretences or hiding, and with fear by our side as a companion but always with us gently holding the reins of our own being.

**The great work of the priestess is an inside job.**

**There is no getting around this work. No spiritual bypassing or denial.**

To truly walk in life and be in service to others as a priestess means to commit to doing the work that is necessary to look at all of our jealousies, bitterness, fears and more. They may be things that others see in you or only you know exist in the recesses of your mind and soul. It's not a public path or work. It's private. And while it may be hard, it's always transformative.

If you want to ignite your soul, you have to go in. You cannot rid or wish your ego away and entirely live from the heart. The things that we so often wish were not a part of us, simply ... *are*. And they are crying out not for our denial, but our attention and love. We all want to live from the heart, but we cannot bypass our mind, thoughts, emotional and cerebral thoughts and needs in doing so.

And along this path when we refuse to keep wounding ourselves over and over again or ignoring the wounds we have, we will stop wounding each other. We will look at our internalised oppressions, our stories, our frailties and so much more and we will take responsibility for what we are going to do about them from a singular moment onwards. We will take a radical, sovereign and powerful stance that we will not project ourselves onto others or blame them for who we are.

Your greatest healing work will heal those around you.

I am still on this path as a messy, imperfect, flawed human being.

*Come walk with me ...*

> *Goddesses:*
> *Cerridwen (Celtic), Ereshkigal (Mesopotamian), Hecate (Greek), Hella (Norse), Nephthys (Egyptian), all winter and crone goddesses*

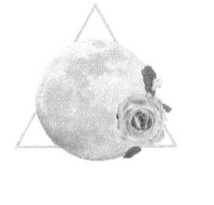

# Learning From the Monkey

We all have an ego and ego voice. We all have a mind monkey.

Some call it our inner critic. Some our inner mean girl or guy. It doesn't really matter what you call it as long as you recognise it is a part of you and is therefore of your own being. I've heard people speak about their ego in such a way that it is not them. And while it may not be the true them, it is a part of who they are. Therefore, we must take responsibility for it. We cannot externalise our ego as something not of ourselves, or our ability to take responsibility for it.

Responsibility means to 'respond with ability'.

How's that for revolutionary? I choose to respond with ability to myself and all I say, feel and think, and do not say, feel, or think. I respond to myself with ability. Who else can do it if not me? I do not blame myself, rip myself to shreds, tear myself apart and knock myself down no matter what I say, feel or think, or do not say, feel or think. I just deal. I respond with ability. I take responsibility. And more often than not I have found that responding with ability to our ego and nasty inner critic begins with truly understanding that what it—what we—tell ourselves is not the truth. That it is a portal to the real truth of our soul voice, but not truth itself.

I have come to see my ego for what it is. And maybe my version of what I believe my ego is and how I have come to see it, will be powerful for you too.

My ego is a voice of my own creation that takes me away from my soul essence.

It is something that tests me, challenges me, creates fear, distracts me, compares me to others, lies to me about my worthiness, propels me into procrastination, assumes, tells me that others do not like me and so much more. It is my own inner voice that has been created by me as one of my greatest personal teachers. It is not my enemy despite what it tells me. It is not to be feared, adhered to, obeyed or blindly believed. It is a messenger that calls me deeper into my truest self. It is a gateway and a door to my highest self.

My ego shows me where I need to care for myself more. How to discern. What is truth and what is false. How I am thinking and showing up in the world versus how I truly want to be. Where I am distracted. How I am spiritually bypassing. Where I am submitting rather than surrendering. How I judge myself. Where I hurt and how I hurt myself.

And in showing me these things my ego opens up a portal for me to see myself through loving eyes, beyond its fears and lies, and it brings me back to the true essence of my soul. By seeing it for what it truly is and accepting it as a part of myself I can then be in compassionate control of understanding why my ego is there, and why I hear it and can be hurt by it. Only then can I know how to change and transcend beyond its mumbles, niggles and roars.

I have learned to know that when my ego:

- ☆ tells me I am not good enough, that it is sending me a challenge to deepen my relationship with myself.
    **Not that I am not good enough.**
- ☆ fills me with fear, that I am being called to ask myself how much I want something and what I am willing to do to make it happen.
    **Not that I should not do something.**
- ☆ tells me I cannot do something, that I am being called to feel into my own power and sovereignty.
    **Not that I am weak and cannot fulfil my own desires.**
- ☆ tells me that I am unlovable, that I am being sent a reminder that my self-love and belief cup is not full, and I must tend to myself.
    **Not that I am unlovable.**
- ☆ tells me that I must be perfect, or I am a failure, that I am whole and can never fail when I live with authenticity and heart, which will include making mistakes.
    **Not that I must live according to a back-breaking version of perfect.**

**Do your ego and inner critic tell you such things too? And maybe more? We are rowing in that boat together, sister. All of us.**

Your ego may tell you things you don't like and don't want to hear, but as it does so, can you see how it can become one of your greatest teachers and is not your enemy? That you are not your enemy and are in fact your greatest teacher? If you ignore it or try to shove it down further into your shadow and darkness, that is where it will spread and gain power.

However, when you truly peel back the deeper meaning through its voice and learn what you are trying to tell yourself, calling yourself to, and loving yourself to even deeper levels for, you will change your life in the most extraordinary way and open yourself up to your full spiritual power. You will see your ego as an ally and teacher that has messages for you that contain powerful keys to your healing and growth.

> *Goddesses:*
> *Kuan Yin (Chinese), Mother Mary (Christian), Tara (Buddhist)*

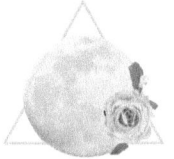

# Being Perfectly Imperfect

Letting go of patriarchal notions of being perfect will be one of our greatest liberators both individually and collectively.

We have forgotten the power and even the fun in embracing mess. In getting dirty and being dirty. We don't allow ourselves to make mistakes and we rarely allow others to do it too. Our non-belief in allowing ourselves to be imperfect makes us come top-down on others. If I need to be perfect then you sure as hell will be too, with anything less than perfection being unacceptable.

A spiritual path is a messy one. That is if it's true and real. If you're not on your knees crying for hope, or forgiveness, or to be guided out of something semi-regularly, you're not really in it. And there is no one way to be spiritual or live spiritually. There is no perfect and no binary, no matter what the latest guru or self-help teacher tries to tell you. Your right way of spiritual being and service will surely involve missteps, heartaches, boundary pushing, tears, fears and moments where you are far from perfect. And therefore beautiful in your imperfection.

I truly believe that so much of our desire to be perfect is internalised misogyny due to the patriarchal world we live in. There is this pervasive ideal, driven especially by powerful white men through politics, business, education and the media that women must be exemplary, refined, together, straight, small, delicate, yielding. That we must be perfect within the realm of what we are told is perfection.

It's an impossible ideal to live up to and in many instances, it is killing us, robbing us of joy, and promoting the turning of woman against woman. So often without even realising we are judging other women for the way they dress, their choice of partner, how much they drink, how much they weigh, how they parent, their choice to not be a parent and so much more.

**This is not freedom. This is not a free life.**

We have the power to stop imposing such perfection on ourselves and others. We can give an almighty finger to the patriarchy by saying 'no more'. You do not get to define what is right and ideal for me or us. I get to define that. We get to define that. And it involves no perfection. We want to embrace our messiness and dirtiness and mistakes and learn from that space and place when we do. We reject remaining pristine, skimming the surface and hiding our mistakes away in an attempt for no one to see or judge us, or to uphold your notion of what we should be.

And know this when you do, sister, embracing our imperfections is not easy.

No one wants to fall over. No one wants to get hurt.

And no one necessarily wants others to see our darkness that may show us to be vain, bossy, controlling, needy etc. I say such things as an example of exactly what I am! And the more I have said and owned that I am such things, the more I have been able to transcend and move beyond them. Go figure! However, what if we made it okay if we and they did?

How might that change *everything?*

How might that help us so deeply with fear and conversely courage as well? How might we take more risks, say 'what the hell' more, give things a go, put ourselves out on a ledge, give up the binary that we will fail and therefore be a failure?

How might things change for us if we allowed the making of mistakes to be okay and that we gently witness ourselves and others while doing so, cheering ourselves and them on for having the imperfect messiness and belief in ourselves to fall over, learn, get back up and that we will be okay?

*It will change everything.*

---

*Goddesses:*
***Bastet (Egyptian), Elpis (Greek), Felicitas (Roman), Mo'o (Polynesian)***

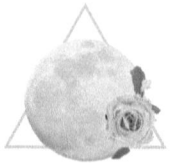

# Your Judgy Pants Don't Fit Anymore

Many of us have developed a deep attachment to judgement. We think, speak and act towards others—and yes, ourselves—in a way that is hypercritical, steeped in nitpicking and searching for faults.

Imaginary yardsticks abound by which we think we and others need to measure up, and that if we don't, that somehow means we are not good enough. And so often it seems we wield these sticks as a weapon to one-up ourselves, put others down, or make sure we are more 'okay' than someone else.

This is mightily supported by social media. It's become so easy to zing out a quick retort, opinion or judgement on something we see posted online, which, of course, always has a human face and heart behind it. Even if we fail to recognise that at the time. Quick jabs. Throwaway lines. Unsupported opinions that we claim as fact and passing judgement on others which could be anything from what they are wearing, how they parent, to a business decision they have made.

It's important to know that we all have an inner judge and that it can be helpful to us. When our inner judge is not driven by our ego it helps us make good decisions, be clear with our boundaries, and avoid people or circumstances that we know are not right for us. Our inner judge also allows us to bring our values and beliefs to life by being able to evaluate when we know things are wrong so that we can be a part of addressing and eradicating injustices such as racism, transphobia, ableism, environmental destruction and more.

There is an enormous difference however between the making of a judgement that is in service to ourselves and others and being judgemental. When we make judgements in service our mind is considered and thoughtful. When we are judgemental, we are reactive, imbalanced, even defensive. Even if we don't consciously realise it. We are in a mode of self-righteousness and avoidance of our shadow, using judgement to project our 'stuff' onto others.

At the heart of being judgemental is how we feel about ourselves. By finding fault or something to condemn in others, we protect ourselves and avoid our own needs. Some may say faults, but I think they are the same. And so, the more we work towards becoming accepting of our entire selves—faults, needs, darkness and all—the more accepting and less judgemental we will be of others.

Releasing judgement as a priestess is a journey of self-acceptance and allowing ourselves the space for all that it means to be human. The letting go of perfectionist standards and binaries, to step into a place that is expansive and graceful, but also messy. Such is the path we go on when we commit to wholly owning ourselves for who we are and who we are becoming.

---

### Goddesses:
*Astraea (Greek), Dike (Greek), Kuan Yin (Chinese), Tara (Buddhist)*

# Are You Really Straight?

To live and serve as a priestess means to be in deep alignment and integrity with all that you say you are and do. To live and serve in your full truth.

I am sure, like me, you have had encounters with people where things just did not seem to add up. A saying of one thing but a presentation of another, or actions that did not gel or align. This does not necessarily mean that someone is or was being deliberately deceptive, even though it may have presented itself in that way. It may simply mean that, like so many of us, they are traversing their inner world with much work to be done before they feel fully aligned to express their truth.

And telling or speaking our truth seems like such an easy thing to do. Tell the truth. Don't lie. Our parents teach us this from an early age. And on the whole, I am sure most of us do lie day to day. We don't consciously lie or set out to deceive people. However, we do deceive ourselves. And therefore, at times, others in turn.

We have things to say and we don't for fear of being judged. We want to do things and we don't because of the risk involved. We want to let things go and don't, for fear of hurting people. We want to say no and we say yes. We want to say yes, and we say no. We want to disagree or put forward another point of view and we stay silent. We see things happen we know we should stand up for and we remain seated to maintain our comfort and, at times, our place of power as well.

When you step onto the path of the priestess and desire to live a life as a spiritual leader you will come to face many truths about yourself and how you desire to serve that you may find hard to express. Your truth about who you are and what you believe, may at times, feel like a huge gumdrop in your mouth that clamps your teeth together. This can be especially the case if your life, up to this point in time where you want to express new truths about yourself, is very different from who you have previously been and shown the world.

And yes, others may judge you, and this has certainly happened to me. They may interpret your truth and integrity differently from you. What is true and aligned for you may not be for them and that includes what they see about you. Only you can know if you speak the truth as you know it and feel it.

**There is no universal truth.**

**Everything in our lives and the lives of others is open to interpretation.**

This calls for deep work as a priestess because when someone challenges your truth you can feel like they are entirely challenging who you are and your integrity with it. What could be more confronting than someone saying you are a liar or a fake? Imagine for one moment how many times priestesses past must have had such things laid at them. A questioning of their skills, power and leadership that from the onset of the patriarchy would have grown and grown.

However, someone questioning your truth is not a dismissal of it.

The choice of alignment, integrity and truth as you feel it and know it always rests with you.

> *Goddesses:*
> *Maat (Egyptian), Veritas (Roman), Anahita (Persian), Athena (Greek), Saraswati (Hindu), Benzaiten (Japanese)*

# Don't Be Afraid of the Dark

I guess by now you have realised that ego and shadow work is deeply required work of the priestess. And I would love to encourage you to see this not as something scary, but rather that this is about the parts of you that are calling for your greatest love and healing. What could in fact be more beautiful and honouring than that?

This work requires your radical self-honesty. Anything less means you're skimming the surface and avoiding. This is about a deep turning within, but always with love, compassion, and a desire to see your own wholeness and divinity. And not letting any fear of what you may find—or not find—stand in your way of truly going where you need to.

So much fear, and therefore darkness, came up for me in the early stages of writing this book and it remained prominent at varying stages throughout the whole writing process. I lost my power almost immediately after being told it would be published by a major publishing house. Up until then I felt strong and so inspired by what was to come, and I truly believed I had something of value to share as a practising priestess.

Then I started to turn outward instead of inward. I became concerned with what others would think of me, and in particular, me writing this book. How they would feel about the priestesses I had included and not included? Would people get it? Would they challenge me even calling myself a priestess?

Lots of shadowy things began to pile up and happen to me on all planes of my existence. I began to have physical problems with my dominant hand which made the writing process painful and at times almost impossible. What is this about? What does it mean? Is this a message for me to stop?

Well-known spiritual leaders began to be publicly called out for their racism, spiritual bypassing and mistreatment of Black, Brown, Indigenous and People of Colour in the spiritual and entrepreneurial communities I was a part of. People I had once admired began to crumble before my eyes as their inherent bias and reliance upon white supremacy seeped out of them in monumentally messy proportions. Where was my part in this? Was I doing enough—would it ever be enough—for me to address such things within myself?

Someone I had always had a positive and warm relationship with accused me of mistreating her. I tried to understand and couldn't. Her truth was not mine. We could not come to an understanding together of what had transpired. Our relationship ended.

I began to have people incessantly tag me and call me into things on social media. People I had accepted friend requests from, and should not have, started to message me on high rotation asking questions about my motives for things, what the meaning and reasoning behind my work was, why I did something that I did. I began to feel totally bombarded, overwhelmed and like I was drowning.

I started to question everything to do with the feminine and use of that word. Masculine as well. As more non-binary people stepped into my life and world, I began to question what this all meant to them and whether or not I was being exclusionary and bowing to heteronormativity without even realising it. Was I part of the problem? What would becoming part of the solution look like and possibly take from me?

My sister almost died. My father, nana and stepfather did die. All left me emotionally bereft in different ways and struggling to cope. I had plunged into the depths of my own shadow right at a time when I was meant to be shining and *on* and writing a book.

How inconvenient. How apt.

And so there have been many periods of time while writing these words for you that I have had to look deeply at my own dark thoughts and behaviours and face the reality of what was shown to me. Which was that I was leaking my personal power and sovereignty (badly) with a gross level of self-pity and neediness, and I needed to claim myself back. It was not easy. I had to ask for help, both from myself and others, and for the first time in my priestess path, I entirely surrendered to what allies needed to come to me with no desire for control of who they may be or what form they may take. And it was the dark and crone Welsh goddess of transformation and rebirth, Cerridwen, who came and said, 'I will walk beside you.'

Cerridwen stirred and stirred me in her dark cauldron until She broke me apart, so that I could be rebuilt with greater wisdom and insight on who I was beyond my ego and pain, why I had committed to writing this book, my role in service, and how my shadow was crying for love and attention, not 'blissful' ignorance or denial. We spoke to each other every day and sometimes even in my dreams. My altar became darker as I opened myself to the mystery of what She had for me in her crone wisdom, and therefore what I had for myself.

By the time we finished walking together, along with a lot of kinesiology, coaching, breathwork and body work, I was no longer the woman I was when I first started writing this book. A lifelong tug of war with comparison, people-pleasing and a lack of boundaries had ended. My entire physical presence had changed, along with dyed blonde hair making way for natural greys and silvers and a loss of more than a third of my body weight, something that She told me was no longer mine to own. I released myself from the large publisher I no longer felt was right for holding the soul of this book and Her message and instead chose another that was much smaller, boutique and reverent for me.

And so even though we often grow up feeling afraid of the dark and resisting it at every turn, know that in the depths of what you fear, or wish was not there, is freedom. A deep liberation that can only be found if you say yes to your whole self and not just the parts of you that feel good or garner praise. You may drag yourself in kicking and screaming. And that's okay. You may wake up one day and finally feel totally ready to go and be excited about it. And that's okay too.

Just go. Listen to the signals. Feel the pull. Know that there is no coincidence in things that smack you down over and over. Ask for help and journey companions. But know that you've got this and whatever you may find and need to heal. And you've got you too. All of you.

---

*Goddesses:*
*Cerridwen (Celtic), Isis (Egyptian), Kali (Hindu)*

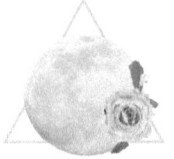

# Beyond Love and Light

Spiritual bypassing is a very real thing.

Psychotherapist, teacher, and author John Welwood coined the term 'spiritual bypassing' for when we use spiritual ideas, practices or beliefs to avoid our own issues, wounds and needs. I liken it to placing a pretty veil over something that we want to hide or pulling a curtain so that something cannot be fully seen. We may totally realise we are doing it and do it anyway. Or we may not have any conscious idea we are doing it at all. It is a form of avoidance to escape or deny the reality of what is really happening for ourselves or others.

Many people choose to bypass their full range of emotions and therefore the full human experience with it. They 'love and light' many things, or even everything, away, when such a response is not only diminishing of their own and others' emotions, needs and lived experience. It is dangerous as well, as is anything that is not steeped in truth.

And it can look on the surface to be exactly the 'right' thing to do and even beautifully and spiritually seductive.

> 'Don't be angry. That won't get you to the answer you need.'

But it actually might. And not allowing people to experience the full range of emotions they need to is a form of spiritual bypassing.

> 'We are all one. There is no difference between us.'

Yes, we are, but we are different too. And not seeing those differences is a form of spiritual bypassing.

> 'Love is the only answer.'

No it's not; sometimes it's food, money, a second chance, an entire ripping down of an oppressive system. And denial of such realities with a veil of so-called love is a form of spiritual bypassing.

> 'We all have the same access to anything we want. I believe in you!'

No, we don't. And believing that we do negates the lived experience of people dealing with deeply rooted structural inequalities every day. And is a form of spiritual bypassing.

Life is not all love and light.

We can wish it was for ourselves or others as much as we want, but it will still never be that way. There are injustices, abuses and soul-crushing power dynamics in the world that we all must traverse as human beings, some of us much more so than others. There are people walking through life with intersecting oppressions that deeply impact their ability to be safe and treated humanely, find meaningful and prosperous work, love who they choose to love without fear, and gain access to healthcare and other supports they need to thrive and be joyful. There is no 'loving and lighting' such things away. Denial of reality harms everyone.

Our desire to avoid pain and even just discomfort can see us bypass 'unpleasantness' in an instant. And we don't only do it for ourselves—we often do it for others as well—even if they don't want us to. Few of us feel comfortable allowing other people, especially those we may love and care for, to sit with discomfort and pain. Our pull to want to feather things away, or try to bypass them as something they are not, is strong.

We can do better than that and as priestesses we must. We have the power to be unconditionally in the messy middle of any of life's experiences such as loss, grief, change and death, and allow others to be so as well. This is what it means to sit in and be with truth. To know that you and those around you on your spiritual path can move through something and come out the other side with what is needed. We can be of comfort to ourselves and others in so many ways that does not involve sweeping something away.

Know that there is infinite power in every part of you and that there is never a need to brush away what you are truly feeling or experiencing, or do it for anyone else either. Spiritually bypassing something, or even your entire self through denial of your shadow, is more dangerous and harmful than anything you could possibly find within there. Put down the veil. What is beyond it is your messy, beautiful, challenging and illuminating truth.

***Goddesses:***
***Veritas (Roman), Metis (Greek), Sága (Norse)***

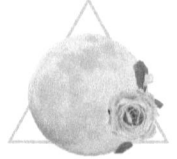

# The Fear of Fear

I think we've reached a point where we fear fear itself. More than, in fact, what we may have been afraid of in the first place. We've come to think that feeling fear, experiencing it and even just thinking about it is bad, and that even the mention of it means something in our lives is not right. However, nothing could be further from the truth.

Fear is, and can be, if we allow ourselves to see it as such, liberatory. A time of transformation. Self learning. Uncovering. A call to bold action and being renewed.

Every time our ego fills us with fear, we cannot believe what it presents is the absolute truth, or react by doing or not doing something, rather we need only act or not from our truest desire. We also cannot pretend it doesn't exist or feels real for us, and that we may experience negative feelings and swirling emotions as a result. At the first feel of fear we must have the courage to admit, even just to ourselves, 'Okay, I'm shaking here. This is raising some fear for me. This is not a bad thing. I've got this and can work through what is really going on.'

How might your life change if when you had fear arise you did not automatically assume that it was bad or something bad was about to happen? How might your life change if you saw fear as a companion in your life and something we all naturally experience from time to time? How might your life change if you saw fear as a sign that you are on the precipice of something incredible and you're being called to make a leap to the next level of you? How might your life change if you saw fear as a powerful call to action? How might your life change if you saw fear as a construct of your own making that was opening you up to your true soul voice and essence?

Women of the ancient world would have lived and died in fear almost constantly. Like, all the time actual adrenalin-pumping, *Am I going to get out of this alive?* fear. Bears, battles, burnings alive. Today, however, so much of our fear is a result of our own thinking, our assumptions, not living in the present moment and future tripping about things that are yet to happen. If they ever will.

If you desire to be a spiritual leader and priestess, fear may always be a part of that path. You cannot invest in your own spiritual and sacred leadership without, as you now know, feeling into your darkness where fear often resides.

Instead of it gripping you, how about you grip it? Shake it and yourself. See it for what it truly is and yourself. Use its power and yourself. Own it and yourself.

Make fear your ally not your enemy and watch how you can truly align with it and the call to action it brings you to be more powerful. And don't surprise yourself if you reach a point where you begin to welcome fear in for the truly powerful gateway it is to a stronger and more sovereign you. When you do, you're really in a place where you and your ego are aligned for your highest good, so much so that it will know its duty to you is to retreat and quieten so that your heart and soul voice can truly step forth.

---

*Goddesses:*
*Hella (Norse), Mazu (Chinese), Morrigan (Celtic), Kali (Hindu), Mami Wata (African), Sekhmet (Egyptian)*

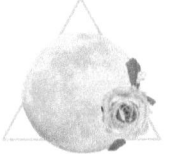

# Our Stories of Loneliness

Have you ever felt lonely?

I think most of us have at some point in time. Maybe many times. I know I have.

Despite the fact that we may be surrounded by people, we can feel disconnected from each other and ourselves too. Alone. Even though it may appear through our seeing eyes that we aren't at all.

One word of 'no' to an invitation and we crumble. A social media post that fails to get the views we want causes our heart to hurt. A blog we write or video we create that does not have the impact we desire, and we feel entirely unseen. An event we host that doesn't sell well makes us question our entire being. We then convince ourselves we are not liked or wanted or loved. That we are destined to do things alone or not at all. That no one gets or sees us.

However, we are never really alone and a path as a priestess will help you to not only understand this but embrace it deeply.

I came to understand that my own personal feelings around loneliness had to do with my disconnection from the Great Mother, and therefore myself. The founder of the School of Shamanic Womancraft, Jane Hardwicke Collings, in an episode I interviewed her for on *The Priestess Podcast*, quite literally scoffed at the thought that as human beings we 'go to nature'. Instead, Jane's impassioned plea was for us to understand that we are nature, intrinsically woven together through time, cycles, birth, life, death and so much more. That we are one and that She as our Divine home and protectress lives just as much within us as we are surrounded by Her every day.

And it was not until my time journeying with the School of Shamanic Womancraft, particularly when I was on a solo wilderness experience alone for three days and three nights in the bush, that I came to know with absolute certainty that I had experienced my last ever feelings of loneliness. Those three days and nights I was entirely alone. No one to talk to. No phone. No radio to natter away in the background. No net to surf. No book to read. No other human being in sight.

And yet as the hours and days crept by with no other human comfort or even food to distract or numb myself with, I heard Her for the first time. At first it was just Her usual sounds more amplified with no other distractions to capture my attention. Birds. Rustling trees. Small drops of rain hitting dry leaves.

Then She began to growl. Low and deep from Her underbelly. A rumbling that called me deeper into Her, calling me to lay on the ground and feel Her with my bare body. I felt both lighter and weaker as my quest continued. And by the third day, alone with no sustenance but water, Her muffled rumblings turned to clear, precise and beautiful words that I knew were for me. As I lay on Her lush forest floor with the sun streaming on my face, She said to me:

> You are never alone. Every morning when you put your feet on the ground, I will be there to hold you. When you are hungry or thirsty, my food and water are yours. When you need shade, I give you my trees. Know with certainty you can always take another breath and I will fill your lungs with air. And that my flowers are your flowers as a reflection and reminder of your beauty. You are never alone. I am you. You are me. I love you unconditionally and without judgement. You are never alone.

I do not know how long I lay there. Time became infinite for me, and when I rose and came back into my body, I felt tears on my face from such a profoundly beautiful and divine awakening. I was changed. And yet more myself than ever before. From that moment on—years ago now—I felt stronger and more sovereign than I ever had. And still do.

I now know deep in my bones that I am never alone. And that neither, sister, are you.

Any sense or thought of loneliness I may feel is a construct of my own ego. Even if I was to be in my final years alive on my own. Even if I was to die on my own. That is the level of surety I have about this now. About how She will always be there for me and is with me.

As the greatest goddess of all our Earth Mother loves us unconditionally with all our faults and failings. Her compassion is infinite. Her wisdom limitless. Her power almighty. Her regeneration way beyond our own. I never question Her. She never questions me. She has no judgement for who I am or what I do. She simply is. And She loves me.

**As She loves you.**

You are never alone. You don't need to walk on Her shores, touch Her trees or play in Her gardens to be with Her. She is a part of who you are. The more you go to Her and do these beautiful things with and as Her, however, the more deeply you will connect and come to honour Her and yourself in all your power, beauty, wisdom and wildness together.

Would your life change if you knew you were always held and loved unconditionally in this way? What would you honour more deeply or commit to if you knew you would always be loved with such grace and power?

As a priestess your relationship with Her is your relationship with yourself.

**You are never alone.**

---

*Goddesses:*
*The Great Mother, All Nature goddesses*

---

# The Goddess Sees All

One of the most powerful ways that you can get to know your inner self is through connecting and working with the goddess.

This is of course what so many ancient priestesses did on their spiritual paths and was central to their lives in every way. And, even though that may not be the way we wish to serve or work with the goddess today, I find it incredible that at any time of our choosing we can connect with the same goddesses that ancient priestesses once did to heal ourselves, ask for guidance, tap into our inner power and so much more.

How we do this, what it may feel like, and even what the goddess may look like has a rather singular portrayal in the modern world, and deconstructing that before you step into Her world is vital. You could be forgiven for thinking given how She is portrayed in everything from art to music to social media, that connecting with the goddess means you're about to enter a world that is all about beauty, flowers and light.

And it may just be that for you, as it was in the beginning for me. However, if you continue to connect deeply and truly to the goddess, while She may show you your light to begin with, eventually please know, She will take you dark. Where you will go only you and She will know. And that's not something that can be predetermined or controlled.

I have a wholly untested and unscientific theory that there is a little bit of the trickster—which is really just crone wisdom—in all goddesses. It is the part of Her that will show you something to tease or distract you, only to then show you the more challenging side of what you *really* need to see.

She will help you to feel comfortable and content, only to then rip that stable rug right out from underneath you so you are forced to see who you truly are and how you manage difficult times. She will illuminate all your light and what is beautiful and shining within you, but then—if you keep working with and calling Her into your life—She will hold a mirror up to you that may be filled with images you do *not* want to see. She will guide you straight into your shadow and those parts of you that are not fully healed.

Why? Because She wants you to feel and live as a whole, healed and divine woman. She wants you to know all of you. Especially the parts of you that you do not want to acknowledge or see. As your ally and guide, She takes a human form as the part of yourself that, at any given time in your life, you most need. She is infinite in Her wisdom and what you need.

**She makes no mistakes.**

---

*Goddesses:*
*All*

# Who Stole My Flower Crown?

When I first started to work more deeply with the goddess, I was in raptures with how She came to me and what She helped me to unfold. The first goddesses that I worked with were the goddesses of love, beauty and sensuality, Aphrodite and Freyja. They felt so divine and gorgeous. They hit me straight in the heart and I fell in love with them. They inspired me to surround myself with flowers, soft colours and candles, and to work on creating feelings and connections for myself that amplified my self-love, self-care and confidence.

I never wanted them to leave me, and even though I know they are always with me in some way, eventually they did leave, stepping away from the very prominent role they played in my life. We reached a point together where I felt the most beautiful, self-loving and confident I ever had been, and they started to fade. I would expect to receive wisdom from them in meditation, or when asking them a question and they would speak so softly I could barely hear them and then they stopped coming all together.

I didn't know that the more I dived into my light and all the things they allowed me to shine and accept in myself—how I cared for other people, made things around me beautiful, supported others to feel their own beauty—the softer they would become. This was a genuine lesson in itself where I had to learn that they were not outside of me but inside. They were me. And I could call on that part of myself at any time I wanted to get the love, power or answer I needed. As can you.

As Aphrodite and Freyja began to leave me, I started dreaming a great deal more in my sleeping hours at night. A dark and indistinguishable figure kept appearing to me. I could never see a clear face, but I knew She held the energy of a female form. Every time She appeared, I would try to get Her to leave or run from Her which quite literally made me sweat in my sleep. She would make my heart race and I would wake with feelings of fright and worry swirling around me.

She kept coming to me, almost every night, for months. Until I 'woke up' to the fact that it seemed the more I resisted Her the more strongly She would come. And so, after She appeared to me again in a dream, the following morning for the first time in more than a year since I had started working at a deeper level with the goddess, I entirely stripped my altar back. All flowers removed. My little Aphrodite statue packed away. My mandala for Freyja disassembled. A swathe of rose quartz crystals taken down. I left only a candle on the table and asked the figure in my dreams to show Herself to me. That I was ready for Her.

And even though I knew in my heart that She was my shadow coming to me as the Dark Goddess, my resistance to Her and feeling the goddesses of Love step away from me felt like a loss. I didn't really want Her to come. I didn't really want to do the work. Which She laughed at and told me in a very clear voice: 'You asked for this. You called me. I am here at your doing.'

She opened up for me where I was not in alignment or full personal integrity in a number of areas of my life and that I had much ego and deeper soul work to do. She told me that She was going to walk with me and that there would be no more illusions, veils or niceties between us. That if I wanted to transform and alchemise the darkest parts of myself this was to be the commitment.

And in trusting Her—this dark and forbidding goddess—I came to know myself deeply and most likely for the very first time. All of me. And especially the parts of me I never wanted to acknowledge. She never did tell me Her name. She didn't need to. I knew She was the entire energy and power of all the Dark Goddesses of time; a wayshower of my shadow and all I needed to transcend.

However you may choose to connect and work with the goddess, know that it will not be all rainbows and flowers. There will be times if you continue on this path of uncomfortableness and stretch, even sadness. All of it is a part of the alchemy of your soul as a spiritual leader and priestess.

She's got you. And that means you've got you too.

---

*Goddesses:*
*All*

# I'm So Sorry

We have all done things we needed, or still need, to say sorry for. And being aligned with a spiritual path in life as a priestess does not make us immune to this. Such is one of the outcomes of not being perfect. We make mistakes, hurt people, stuff things up, have regrets, wish we could take something back and likely do such things more than once to the same person or people.

And it's likely that we need to say sorry and be forgiving most of all to ourselves. At least in the first instance. And that until we do that for ourselves, we likely will continue to do things that mean we need to be in deep apology to others.

We all carry burdens for things we have done that maybe others know about or don't. We have all lied and hurt and betrayed people, even when we did not mean to. And even sometimes we may have meant to. This is a normal part of being a messy and flawed human being and I don't believe any of us are immune. Including me.

Hopefully either at the time of our transgression we apologised sincerely, or at a later time when we realised. And then comes the part about what we may need to do to forgive and say sorry to ourselves for what transpired as well. Which is often the part we forget, or simply don't know is an important part of the full circled nature of how saying sorry and forgiveness can be so powerful.

How much is the fear we carry now potentially related to us not fully forgiving ourselves for things we have done or not done? What do we need to work through for radical realignment as well as releasing judgement so that we can continue our journey to wholeness as a human being? What burdens are we carrying that hold us back from the spiritual inner path of the priestess such as putting ourselves first, being still, releasing control, stepping into the power of our shadow and so much more?

What may happen if you forgave yourself? If you wrapped yourself in a soft cloak of gentle and healing sorry for everything that has come before you that required you to do so? How may it open you up to new awareness, insight and love that will deepen your spiritual path and ability to powerfully lead?

Saying sorry can be, and often is, deeply healing for someone who needs to hear it. Don't forget that you can be that healer for yourself too. And that often we are the most significant person we owe that apology to for all the times we allowed our ego and fear to guide us away from the true nature of our soul.

---

*Goddesses:*
*Kuan Yin (Chinese), Tara (Buddhism), Clementia (Roman),*
*Rhiannon (Celtic)*

# Alignment

I came to realise that a large part of my priestess path was not in alignment a few years ago when it came to my relationship with the Great Mother. My truth is I've always been an inside gal and still am. A reader, cosy fire dweller and cat-in-lap lover, much more than a wild hiker or windswept-beach walker.

However, I came to realise that if I was to ever truly feel deeply connected to Her land I live on, the seasons She gifts me with and the sheer majesty of Her life force, I needed to spend more time with Her. I needed to get to know myself in the truth of my relationship with the Greatest Goddess of all with nothing else except Her and me.

And like so many things I have found as a priestess, when I have been called to do something, I am intensively called in such a way that goes deep beneath the surface. Deep beneath the surface to my truth. I consciously began to put myself with Her on a more regular basis and then decided to undertake a year-long journey in the Otway forests with the School of Shamanic Womancraft.

It was intensely raw, challenging and wild. And at times, She was brutal in what felt like Her force but was in fact Her love. Blinding rain. Blistering cold. Searing heat. Leeches as large as your fist. (*Not* joking!) Wild boars. Raging mosquitoes. And not a creature comfort in sight. No phone at end of hand. No comforting family love. No warm water. No soft bed.

But amongst Her harshness—Her own truth which She has no issue speaking—was Her gentleness and beauty. Glistening dew on eucalyptus leaves at dawn. Sunlight streaming through lush bracken. Petite pockets of wildflowers. The joyous cackle of kookaburras at the most divinely timed moment.

Deepening into Her. It changed me and how I feel about and relate to Her. But it is still a journey for me. A work in progress.

If you are out of integrity in any way as a priestess, know that the more you connect with the Divine and Goddess, the more She will pull you back into line. Nothing will come to you that is not the truth and that includes if you get smacked about and sent messages that you need to get your alignment sorted. Let Her do this for you and keep searching for and living your truth as you see it.

You do not need a permission slip from anyone to live as you are called and to know the truth of who you are and why you are here. To seek that is to give up your truth for another.

---

**Goddesses:**
*Sophia (Greek), Aletheia (Greek), Fides (Roman)*

# You First, Priestess

To live as a priestess means to craft a life that first and foremost honours yourself.

How would your life change if you did that? If you truly put yourself first and resisted any notions of being self-centred or vain or self-serving. A life where you saw yourself as reverent and Divine. To be in deep service to others requires you to do this. To be this.

We can take so much inspiration from ancient priestesses who first honoured themselves and were seen as vessels of the Divine. Before the onslaught of warring tribes and the patriarchy, women in general, let alone priestesses and those seen as spiritual leaders, were revered. Seen as Divine. Sacred. Beautiful. A part of the incredible fabric of life itself as givers of life, healers of the sick, knowers of the moon and the Great Mother, and gentle ushers of moving beyond the veil once death has descended. They took care of themselves as they did others because they knew they had to, to carry out their duties.

Modern living, let's face it, has us pretty burnt out. More women than ever are living with adrenal fatigue, anxiety and exhaustion.

We're fried. Instead of someone else burning us like women of our ancestral past, we're doing it to ourselves and allowing modern life to grip and burn us, rather than fire us up. And I've been there and have to constantly watch this for myself. I'm a woman, daughter, wife, stepmother, business owner, creative, coach, trainer, podcast host, writer, speaker, space holder, priestess and, and, and. That comes with a price, as I am sure it does for you, if I don't consciously commit to putting myself first.

We often say we need time out, but what if instead we consciously crafted a life that we did not need to take time out from? One where we were always taking exquisite care of our own spiritual, emotional, psychological and physical needs. Where we were always lusciously and reverently full and giving from the overflow of our own self-care. Radical self-care and love are not only, or even ever, about bubble baths and massages. They're about things like setting—and sticking to—boundaries, saying no, following your intuition when all around you may say the opposite, consciously curating who you spend time with, honouring your anger and rage and being vulnerable to love and be loved.

We've twisted self-care into a capitalist and patriarchal notion that keeps us on the surface and doesn't encourage us to go deep within. I'm all for a good bath but this is about so, so much more than that.

Are you truly putting yourself first in your life? Are you truly honouring yourself and the precious gift of your life every day? If not, this calling is asking you to do just that.

**Without a moment to lose.**

*Goddesses:*
*Artemis (Greek), Coventina (Celtic), Diana (Roman), Isis (Egyptian), Zywie (Slavic)*

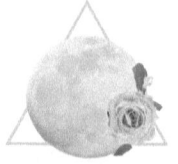

# Her Frequency, Your Power

If the priestess was to have a frequency it would surely be stillness. Stillness to create the conditions required for transmuting things such as our pain, ego and feelings of separateness. Stillness to create the conditions to transform.

We know that priestesses past spent much of their time in silence. Quiet, contemplative prayer, meditation, trance and thought that allowed the goddess to speak to and through them. They embraced and honoured the beauty of stillness so they could truly hear Her voice. So that in turn they could hear their own.

Your inner priestess lives within the most still and deep parts of yourself. Those parts of you that are both gentle and soft, as well as powerful and bold. Those parts where your most sovereign self reigns.

Stillness, silence and solitude need to be your new best friends if you desire to live and serve as a priestess. Hearing what we usually never hear because we are so busy and overflowing not with love, but with worry and stress, however we are living in a world where our true voice is drowned out constantly. We crave noise and often resist silence, even in conversation. We hate pauses and feel uncomfortable with them, when the truth is that is so often where the magic of a moment happens.

Stillness is the great power and 'home' of the priestess. That place and way of being which is still and silent so that the voice of god, goddess and your own soul can be heard.

I encourage you to not place pressure on yourself to meditate or pray to begin with here. Simply learn to be more still and silent. And listen, truly listen, to the divinity of your own soul voice from within, maybe for the first time ever. Sounds easy, right? Maybe not so much.

May the Goddess be with you, sister!

> *Goddesses:*
> *Sige (Gnostic), Danu (Celtic), Sophia (Gnostic)*

## Tingly Trinkets

Spiritual work that calls us in means we have to move beyond, well beyond, any notion that we have to have an arsenal of accoutrements to make that work meaningful or even possible. We don't.

In so many ways we have become hung up on what it means to be spiritual or 'enlightened' and that we must buy all the candles, crystals, oracle cards and chakra sprays that can accompany such journeys. Spirituality has, like so many things in our capitalist world, become commercialised and opportunistic in an attempt to convince us without such things, we will never be able to reach what we are truly searching for and how we can show up in best service as the priestess we may desire to be.

Now don't get me wrong—she says, as she recognises that either you or maybe someone you love has gifted you this book—I love beautiful things. I have an incredibly strong beautifier aspect stemming from my love of Goddess Aphrodite, and I adore making my spiritual devotion and practice as beautiful as I can. A world without candles to me would be a lesser world, especially when I think that they have been used in spiritual ways for more than 5,000 years.

The important thing to know is that such things really are just gateways to the work required and ultimately none of them are truly needed. You don't need candles, goddess statues, meditation sprays or even flowers to reach the divine place and voice of your soul within.

The Great Mother does not charge for you to be with Her. Her ground to sit or lie on in prayer or meditation, is free beneath your feet. You can give yourself the gift of time whenever you want.

And you don't need to buy a thing to make it happen.

---

*Goddesses:*
*The Great Mother, Mother Earth, Mother Nature, Pachamama*
*(Andean), Papatūānuku (Maori), Gaia (Greek)*

# There Is No Road Map

Walking a path as a priestess means being prepared to let go of control of a lot of your life and step into the unknown.

A lot of control.
Maybe control of everything.

You can't know everything or even want to know it when you choose to honour yourself as a spiritual being. You have to be prepared to embrace the unknown and unseen.

Did priestesses past *see* goddesses or did they feel them? Sense their energy? Hear their call and voices? A willingness to sit with the paradox and the unknown, while trusting and allowing the flow of the mystery to be part of the foundation of our lives is deeply required here.

If you think you can control what your priestess path is going to look like, you cannot. If that's what you need to have the courage to step onto the path, it's time to stop now. You can't get it or know. If you want it all laid out before you, no one is going to do that for you. You have to be prepared to go there. This truly is about living in the present moment and not future tripping, worrying or getting anxious about what is to come.

If I had fully known where my priestess path would lead me (or more specifically the very dark and shadowy moments and experiences I've had along the way), I may not have stepped onto the path at all. My naivety had me believe this whole priestess 'thing' was simply going to allow me to indulge my love of flowers, candles, quiet time and being in sacred circle.

And while it has done those things as an iceberg tip, it's also seen me on my knees crying in the darkness, wrestling with my own ego and demons, retreating from family and friends while I worked through so many things, facing constant and ongoing fears about being seen as a priestess and so much more. All par for the course. Of course.

But in my control?
Not in the least.
And I wouldn't have it any other way.

Embrace it. The unknown, the unseen, the untouchable. It's where magic in you lies that you don't or may not even have a name for yet.

---

*Goddesses:*
*Baba Yaga (Slavic), Hecate (Greek), Lilith (Sumerian),*
*Morrigan (Celtic)*

# You Know What To Do

You truly do.

You may often feel as though, as a messy but beautiful woman, you do not know what to do at any given time, but I promise, dear heart, you do. You are your greatest knowing and wisdom source in life.

And you don't need to crowdsource your life on Facebook, constantly ask others what is best for you and turn your life decisions over to the latest self-help or spiritual guru that tries to tell you they have all the answers you need. That's a power grab of the highest order that you do not need to play with. You've got this. You've got you.

Feeling into the power of knowing yourself and what you need takes time. It is a commitment. But the only right answers you will ever receive live within you. You can call on guides and goddesses to help and enable you to light up the answers you seek, but always remember that they are simply a reflection of you. They are you. When a goddess guides you, you guide you. When an angel whispers wisdom to you, you whisper wisdom to you. When a god speaks to you, you speak to you.

This I know for sure.
You are the mistress of your own heart, mind, body and soul.

And if you are lost and have the story playing that you do not know what to do or what you need, or who you are, know, sister, that you do. It may be hiding deep within your shadow or beyond the fearful voice of your ego and or in the depths of stillness you so deeply need. But hiding does not mean gone. It is there. You are there. And if you don't know what you need to know now. You will.

This is what it means to be truly sovereign as a priestess.

To know that you have all you need and are all you need.
That you are sovereign.

This is a lifelong path for me. To know that I do not need the gaze or approval of any other to be okay, and further to that, know that I am okay, exactly as I am in this moment.

Maybe it will be for you too.

If so, I gladly walk with you.

---

*Goddesses:*
*Diana (Roman), Artemis (Greek), Isis (Egyptian)*

# PART V

# Living Embodied

**Let's bring this *priestess* to life.
Let's bring you to life as a priestess!**

Living embodied is all about your life as it looks and feels *every* day living as a modern priestess. This will of course look and feel different for everyone. What feels right and even luscious to you may feel way off for someone else. It's about finding what is most sacred and spiritually beautiful for you.

The following practices and healing paths are just some of the ways you can bring more sacredness into your life. They are what I think are important to the path of every priestess, however there is no bible, manual or rule book here. The Divine will show you the way. In fact, you will show you the way by listening to and responding to your highest self as you read them. You will always know best.

These sacred practices and ways of being are inspired by ancient priestesses and practices past, and bought into context for modern living. Some will likely resonate with you more deeply than others, and even give you clues as to your deeper level of service as a priestess that is to come for you or is already in motion.

Each one is designed to inspire you to know the unfolding answer to the question: 'How do I *live* as a priestess every day?'

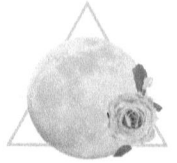

# Sacredness Every Day

Every moment in our lives can be sacred and a teacher to us if we allow it to be. Even the hard stuff or things we don't want to have happen.

You know you're getting things right when you try to find the lesson of grace in things like the dishwasher blowing up right after your big family gathering, a shopping trolley running into the back of your bare ankle, a bird pooping on you in a brand new dress, or getting a stomach bug when you go on holiday.

Such things are of course, small, and even inconsequential in our lives. Especially when so many people have had, or are having experiences that are much worse such as abuse, assault, racism and heart-shattering grief and loss. No human being deserves to have such things happen to them. No person manifests such things happening to them. No person attracts such things happening to them in a deliberate way. It is no one's karmic 'duty' to have to endure such things.

Priestesses honour the sacredness of *all* things and experiences in life.

When I say all, I really do mean all. This does not mean we don't get pissed, cry, whine or feel angry. Such feelings and emotions can be sacred too and so often contain healing powers as well. We can deny them all we want and then so often will see them manifest in another form that makes things harder to deal with. Unexpressed anger can become a dark depression. Unexpressed needs can contribute to deep-seated people-pleasing and anxiety. Unexpressed whining (yes whining!) can set us up to bypass what is really happening in our lives and how we truly feel about something, having us believe we are better to keep quiet, not rock the boat and remain 'neutral', at the expense of our own expression and needs.

It also does not mean we deserve such things when they happen to us or we experience them. This is not about presenting a picture of anyone who isn't afraid to let it all out (um, hello Boudicca, Dahia, and Madame Laveau!) or the spiritually bypassing 'notion' that this is your soul's path and was meant to happen to you. That's a very convenient truth for an oppressor to grab hold of and essentially say 'you deal'.

It's not about that at all, but rather is something that you gently and reverently practise opening yourself to over and over again, especially in moments where life feels hard or harsh. What is the lesson in this for me? How can I find the real meaning here? Is gratitude possible for me right now? Is there something bigger here I need to know?

If you can learn to ask yourself such powerful questions or simply reflect on yourself and your life happenings in a deeper way, then you are truly beginning to bring yourself as a priestess to life.

Couple that with seeing the joy and beauty in everyday living such as doing the dishes, raking leaves, feeding a pet, brewing your tea, or changing your sheets, then your life becomes a series of small moments strung together to make up a beautifully sacred and reverent existence.

# Going Back

Finding out your ancestry and cultural lineage will be one of the greatest gifts you can explore and honour on your priestess path.

For some of us this may be a more simple task than for others. If you are adopted or disconnected from your birth family, it may be difficult for you to extensively explore this aspect of your life and spirituality. And of course, not being able to do so does not mean your spiritual gifts or leadership are incomplete or not whole in any way. You can only work with what you know or are able to find, and your connection to the land you currently reside on or were born on may become of more importance to you.

If you are connected to your birth family, speak to your older family members before you no longer can. Ask them to tell you stories of where they were born, how they played and went to school, whether they went to church or had a spiritual practice, and what they know of their parents and wider family. And if you're very blessed, whether they can tell you anything about their culture and traditions. What were their old ways with food, dance, connection to the earth, traditions, initiations, games, crafts? What were the women in the family like?

What did they do, birth, create, endure? What were the men in the family like? What are their stories?

All are a part of you. Their wisdom and spiritual devotions course through your veins. They are a part of your ancestral DNA and heritage, even if you do not practise or live in the way that they once did.

Exploring my own ancestry and cultural lineage has become an enormous part of my priestess path, especially in relation to coming to terms with the fact that I am a descendant of colonisers and live on unceded land which belongs to the traditional owners of where I reside in Australia, the Wurundjeri People of the Kulin Nations. Committing to knowing the stories of how my ancestors came to be here has become incredibly important to me and learning as much as I can about them and what life and their spiritual practices may have been like before widespread colonisation.

This is still a journey I am on and I am amazed that my research—with a lot of determination thrown in—has allowed me to reach back as far as the tenth century in my family lineage which I now know is predominantly Celtic from England, Scotland, Ireland and Wales, with an interesting streak from Iberia, Greece, Italy and the Balkans. And along the way I inspired a passion for ancestry in Glenn, who has learned, much to his surprise, that he has significant cultural lineage from Scandinavia for which he is now claiming full Viking ownership and the potential he is a descendant of Odin himself! Do not be in the least surprised if your exploration of this area of your life instils in others around you a similar curiosity.

Having a deeper and richer understanding of your own familial ancestry and cultural ties will help you deepen your connection to your own personal history and self, where you come from, the rituals and practices that are a part of who you are and how all of them are available to you as a priestess to practise and work with. It will also hopefully inspire you to know that no matter what your lineage, there will be beautiful and sacred practices, goddesses, rituals, ways with herbs, plants, foods and more that will be special to you and able to be fully practised and honoured by you as well.

This, in turn, allows you to know with confidence that things within your own realm are of your own culture and not others, which you may have inadvertently or blatantly appropriated for your own use and practice, without having any real idea of their origins, or if they are sacred and only to be used by someone from that culture. This is of particular importance if the practice may be an Indigenous one that colonisation and white supremacy have at some point in time, and still now, oppressed the creator or user in some way (even seen them be injured or killed), to now only be claimed by white people as exotic, pretty or desirable for their own use.

Any ties you can find to your past cultural, spiritual and familial lineage will help you to more deeply understand your spiritual leadership and priestessing today. You may not always like what you find or understand it. It's all a part of you in some small or significant way, however, that you can learn from and be inspired by in beautiful and sacred ways that will always have the deepest meaning to you above all others.

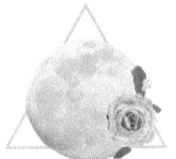

# Take Me to the Altar

Creating your own sacred place as a priestess is a simple but powerful thing to do to honour your spiritual path and work. It can act as an anchor for your gratitude, prayer and stillness, and also bring you great joy and comfort as well.

A personal sacred place can be as simple as a small ornament on your bedside table where you place a candle and a flower in a bud vase. It can be a small collection of crystals and an oracle card in front of your meditation or reading chair. A tiny nook in a corner of your favourite room with a comfy chair, special shawl and essential oils. A special place in your garden that needs nothing more than your loving gaze and presence amongst the Great Mother's gifts. All are altars in their own right.

My altar is a place for me to sit or lie in front of. It is a place of beauty and reflection and a space where I deeply honour myself. Many tears have been shed in front of it. And I also have smiled and laughed in joy as I have prayed for myself and others and called in my deepest wisdom from within. It consists of nothing more than a low bench covered in a throw and whatever candles, statues, oils, flowers or cards I am called to use at any given time.

More often than not my altar is reflective of the current season of the Great Mother. I choose flowers that are in season. Crystals that are reflective of a bright shining summer or a dark cold winter. Oils that support my immune system at that time of year. And always colours that are reflected in nature at the time as well. This works for me and allows me to feel more attuned to Her and my own inner reflections. I have also set altars in honour of particular goddesses, a lunar phase, my blood cycle or archetypal energies I have been working with. There are no rules here. Any physical space that feels sacred to you can be an altar.

**My altar is my most holy and personal space. For me.**

**What it is for you, only you explore and create. As it should be.**

You can also travel with an altar, taking it with you everywhere you go. A small collection of simple but meaningful objects can be taken with you and placed outside your tent, on your hotel dresser, or on a bedside table in a place where you are a guest. I always journey with a travel candle, oracle deck, favourite crystal, and oils or herbs that feel good or necessary to me at the time. It supports me to feel anchored with a small spiritual place for my prayers, meditation and stillness, and also reminds me that we do not need a large or permanent altar space to be connected to our divinity within.

# Passionate Praying

A prayer is an expression of gratitude or a sacred request for help and guidance. Many people think of prayer as only being something that can be asked of God, but it can be asked of any being of your choosing. God, goddess, an angel, a spirit entity that you feel close to or desire to be so. And most definitely a prayer can be asked of or given to the Great Mother.

Prayer and praying don't come with rules. Prayer is something that you can do at any time of the day or night. And at any moment of feeling: joy, confusion, sadness, openness.

When you pray you open up a line of communication to yourself. You open your heart and soul to wisdom that is at once outside of you but also within you. You can do it every day, once a week, whenever you feel like it. But the more you do it the more those lines remain open and that you are likely to hear things of importance to you even when you are not praying. The more you pray the more you make yourself available to be heard.

If you desire to call it something else other than praying, do. I appreciate the fact that for some the words 'prayer' and 'praying' are very attached to religious dogma and even punishment. And so why not reclaim it for yourself in a way that feels right for you? Expressing sacred gratitude or calling in guidance is something for all of us. It shouldn't be something you not do just because you don't like the word 'prayer'.

**Make it a part of your practice and being.
There are words to be heard.**

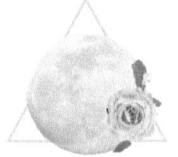

# Intuition Ignition

Your intuition is your ability to be able to feel and understand something without conscious thought or logical reason. It is your instinct. Gut feel. Core truth. Guidance system. Higher intelligence. Inner knowing. Deep wisdom.

It cannot be seen or even at times fully described.
It is a knowing and feeling that is yours alone.

Your intuition as a priestess is one of the most magical things you 'own'. It is always with you, even if you feel it is not strong or even 'working'. It is!

To ignite your intuition and then have it lovingly serve you for life, you must see it as a relationship that requires nurturing and developing. You cannot expect your intuition to become strong and serve you if you don't give it loving time and attention. It needs to know you take it seriously! If you ignore it or don't trust it, it is unlikely to serve you in the powerful way it could. It will always be with you but be hidden under the layers of your ego voice, external influences and opinions of others. And just like any relationship, the more you hear your intuition, and then act lovingly in partnership with it, the more confidence you will have with it and it with you. Intuition will then be more likely to come back to you in service over and over again.

Learning to understand if your ego or intuition is talking to you is key to you feeling more aligned with your intuitive nature. But how do you know the difference, especially if your ego voice and mind chatter is strong? Again, just like any of our relationships, it involves a lot of trust, commitment and discernment. Which can sound rather laborious, but is an exercise in self-love and a deepening of your relationship with the innermost part of you. Therefore, it is always worth it.

Your intuition will always speak to you with kindness and love. It could be a gentle or strong love, a compassionate but insistent kindness, but it won't, unlike your ego, berate you or make you question your worth. It will only ever encourage you in a way that is for your highest good. It may not always make sense to you or be what you want to hear however!

Such is the path to all things that are for your best self. They don't always come packaged in the way you think they will. Despite what your intuition may look, sound or feel like to you—even if odd or new or fantastical—it will never lead you astray. This is of course unlike your ego which can confuse you and make you question yourself. Your intuitive voice and guidance wants you to know joy and love, not fear or worry. If it feels good or at the very least sparks curiosity in you, that's your intuition. If it feels outright worrisome or negative, that's your ego.

And the best way to hear, develop and nurture your intuition is through stillness, silence and reflection. For some it may be meditation and prayer. The gateway to your intuition becoming stronger (and you intuitively with it) is being with yourself, slowing down and taking your time with everything you do. Your intuition can at times speak to you loudly and clearly and you have no trouble hearing it. Many other times, it will be quiet, and by that very nature calling you to sit with yourself in a still, gentle and compassionate way so you can hear it and make loving decisions for yourself as a result.

If you open up to the knowing of your intuition and what it has to guide you with, your path as a priestess will become lit with possibilities. Listening to *its* magic and mystery is listening to *your* magic and mystery. What could be more powerfully guiding in your life than that? Your deepest inner wisdom, calling and message. Beyond your ego. Beyond oppressive or judgemental influences, to the absolute heart and core of who you truly are and why you are here in this lifetime in a role of spiritual leadership.

You can call upon all the guides, goddesses, allies, coaches, mentors and more in your life, and please do, but if they don't lead you back to your own innate wisdom, they are not serving you. You don't need anyone to tell you what to do. You know. And your intuitive nature is the key to unlocking that knowing.

Leaning into and developing a loving and close relationship with your intuition is all about you leaning into and developing a loving and close relationship with yourself. It's the road to being your own best friend and greatest ally. And there is no one more qualified or wise for you to turn to about any decision or path you wish to take in life than yourself.

# Mum's Calling

Stepping onto the path of the priestess also means consciously choosing to develop a deeper relationship with the Great Mother. In fact, any spiritual journey or undertaking we commit to in life will, at some point in time, lead us into greater communion with Her.

As it should. And how can it not?

As our giver and provider of life She is a part of our essence and very being. The air we breathe. The water we drink. The land we walk on. All are from Her and of Her.

Developing a deeper relationship with Her as nature, allows you to develop a deeper relationship with yourself. You will come to see Her as someone and something that does not just nourish you at a surface, but clearly very vital level of air and land, food and water, but as you find divine ways to connect with Her at a soul level, you will come to see and experience Her wisdom, beauty, ferocity, strength, resilience and wildness as a reflection of yourself. That She is you and you are Her. And that you are infinitely connected beyond sight to where your soul resides.

The more you choose to consciously develop and deepen a relationship with Her, the more your way of being as a priestess will be ignited. And how you choose to do this is entirely up to you. What may work for you with Her may not for someone else. It will look different for every person.

You may begin by committing to spending more time with Her away from your desk and indoor world. Walking with Her. Touching Her. Swimming with Her. Climbing Her. Listening to Her. And every day simple things such as gardening, eating seasonally and tending to indoor plants. And it is a given that the closer you choose to be with Her, the more you will see and feel Her beauty and presence, and in turn, that of your own. She will act as a beautiful reflective mirror to you at all times. And if you choose to slow down and listen to Her, She will of course talk to you through birdsong, wave roars, tree whispers, leave crunches and more. She will communicate with you at an even deeper level if you commit to being with Her with no distractions present. No phone required!

Simply spending time with Her, however, is not necessarily going to allow you to develop a deep bond or ongoing relationship where you are in reciprocity with each other. It's a beginning, but as a priestess your calling with Her is to go beyond any surface veil to where Her heart beats and yours does too. This will require you to feel into Her—and therefore yourself—at a deeper spiritual level by doing things such as land based meditations for an hour, a day or even overnight. Creating and conducting ceremonies and rituals in Her honour to give thanks and gratitude. Wandering with Her with no perceived purpose. Nourishing Her with your menstrual blood, prayers and touch. Exploring new ways of being with Her through foraging, bushcraft, finding wild edibles and medicines and so much more.

This is how you cultivate a relationship that honours Her magic and helps you to understand how constantly and deeply She loves you and provides for you. This 'work' and joy as a priestess allows you to take one moment, and then another, another, and another to deeply appreciate and honour Her for all She is and all She gives.

**She loves you.**

**How will you love Her back?**

# The Wheels of the Year Go Round and Round

One of the most rich and beautiful ways you can deepen your relationship with the Great Mother, and yourself, is by honouring Her cycles and seasons through the spiritually potent Wheel of the Year. This ancient honouring and practice provide us with amazing opportunities to reflect and give gratitude for our lives and what is unfolding in them, as a reflection of what is taking place in nature.

The Wheel of the Year is a symbol of the eight seasonal or religious festivals of Neo-Paganism and Wicca.[1] It includes four solar festivals:

>Winter Solstice/Yule
>Spring Equinox/Ostara
>Summer Solstice/Litha
>Autumn Equinox/Mabon

And four seasonal festivals: Samhain, Imbolc, Beltane and Lughnasadh. No evidence has been found that the Wheel was used in ancient times, but the Celts did celebrate festivals at varying times of the Wheel year. The modern-day Wheel of the Year was first suggested by mythologist Jacob Grimm in 1835 and came to be as it is known now by the Wicca movement in the 1950s.

The Wheel of the Year includes the following holy days for both the northern and southern hemispheres:

- ☆ Samhain (31 October/30 April)
- ☆ Winter Solstice/Yule (21-22 December/21-22 June)
- ☆ Imbolc (2 February/2 August)
- ☆ Spring Equinox/Ostara (21-22 March/21-22 September)
- ☆ Beltane (1 May/1 November)
- ☆ Summer Solstice/Litha (21-22 June/21-22 December)
- ☆ Lughnasadh (1 August/1 February)
- ☆ Autumn Equinox/Mabon (21-22 September/21-22 March)

These times support us to focus our attention on the energies of those seasons and give thanks for what we have learned and gained at different times of the year. They encourage us to pause, reflect and express gratitude for what we are receiving, what we may have lost and let go of, and how we are maintaining our own personal harmony and balance.

## Samhain

Samhain marks the beginning of the cycle in the Wheel of the Year. It is what we know today as New Year. Samhain means 'summer's end' and signifies the end of the season of light and the beginning of the season of dark. It is a time to give thanks for what we have received throughout the year and reflect on what we have lost, especially loved ones who have become ancestors. Many rituals related to Samhain are now identified with Halloween. Samhain is also a time when the veil between the living and the dead is believed to be at its thinnest, an 'in-between' time where the dead could potentially move more readily into the realm of the living. It is the perfect time of year to make an altar to your ancestors, speak to them in your prayers and meditations and call forth their wisdom.

##  Winter Solstice/Yule

Yule is the Winter Solstice celebration, honouring the shortest day of the year after which days grow longer. Yule honours the renewing cycles of life, rebirth rejuvenation and growth. Trees were very important at the time of Yule and were considered sacred to the Celts as the homes of deities and spirits. At Yule a tree was decorated outdoors, and a bonfire lit to create a yule log, which symbolised the rebirth of light and new beginnings. People gathered around the log to sing songs and throw a piece of holly, symbolising challenges of the past year, into the flames. A piece of the log was saved to start the next year's fire, symbolising continuity. Gifts were also offered. These symbolic acts we can now see have been adapted into the Christian celebration of Christmas.

##  Imbolc

Imbolc is the mid-way point between the Winter Solstice and Spring Equinox, and is a time of rebirth and purification. Associated with pregnancy, Imbolc also has strong links to fertility, hope and the promise of the future, concepts which were embodied in the Celtic goddess Brigid. Imbolc celebrations involved weaving dolls of Brigid and making sun wheels from corn stalks representing fertility, continuity, luck and the life principle of fire. Imbolc is a wonderful time to engage in nature craft, light a fire and gather friends, and visit a natural water source to complete a cleansing ritual.

## Spring Equinox / Ostara

Ostara is the celebration of the Spring Equinox, named after the Germanic spring goddess Eostre. It symbolises the return to light after winter and is a time of balance, creativity and renewal. Ostara is associated with the fertility symbols of rabbits, eggs and chicks, and was observed in ancient times with celebratory feasts. Flowers are also a much loved and traditional symbol of this budding springtime. Filling your altar or house with fresh flowers, planting seeds, creatively brainstorming a new project and spring cleaning are wonderful things to do at the time of Ostara.

## Beltane

Beltane celebrates light, fertility and the coming of summer. Bonfires played an important role at Beltane where they were believed to represent someone's passion and desires. Dancing was an integral part of Beltane and this often took place around a tree or the phallic symbol of the maypole. As dark days gave increasing way to light ones, it was believed that all of nature including faeries and sprites awoke. Beltane is a beautiful time to undertake any goddess ritual that honours your sacred feminine, conduct a fire ceremony, dance, give an offering to the fae folk or engage in a pleasure ritual.

## Summer Solstice / Litha

Litha celebrates the longest day of the year at the Summer Solstice. It is a turning point of the year when the days become shorter. The sprites and faeries awoken at Beltane were believed to be in full strength at Litha and had the greatest potential to cause mischief or harm. It was therefore very common for self-protection rituals to be conducted at Litha during ancient times as well as lighting bonfires, dancing and eating fresh fruit and honey cakes. Litha is a wonderful time to be outdoors with the Great Mother basking in the sun, swimming, wildcrafting and talking with friends and family while watching the sun set.

## Lughnasadh

Lughnasadh is a harvest festival which is celebrated at the half-way point between summer and autumn. The first fruits of the harvest in ancient times were offered to the gods and goddesses with much feasting, songs and games. Lughnasadh is a wonderful time of reflection as we honour all that summer and the bright shining nature of that period has given us. It is the perfect time to write a gratitude list, volunteer, go for long walks outdoors, surround your altar and self with warm harvest colours and eat nature's abundance, especially fruit, bread and corn.

## Autumn Equinox / Mabon

Mabon celebrates the Autumn/Fall Equinox and is a time of giving thanks and deep reflection for what one has gained and lost over the past year. Ancient Mabon rituals focused on the loss of the goddess who goes into the underworld in autumn/fall and does not return until spring. Almost every ancient civilization had a story involving a goddess or god who undertakes this journey and with their returning brings great prosperity, abundance and life at spring. Mabon is a beautiful time to decorate your altar in autumn/fall colours, conduct a balancing ritual or meditation to honour the equal parts of the day and night at this time, leaf craft, invite into your space the Dark Goddess with approaching winter and give deep gratitude for all the past year has given you.

While the Wheel of Year as it is today is quite a modern construct, its honourings, traditions and rituals are ancient, especially with the acknowledgement and celebration of life and time as a never-ending and repeating cycle. The holy days then, as now, support us to live seasonally, remain balanced and become more aligned with the Great Mother as we seek meaningful ways as priestesses to honour ourselves at potently rich times of the year.

# Luna Love

Since the time of the ancients the moon has played a pivotal role in our spiritual lives. Many ancient cultures observed the cycles and patterns of the moon believing it to be especially connected to the goddesses and gods. One only has to dive into the world of the Goddess in particular to see how many of them are deeply associated with the moon. In ancient times, the moon also guided a significant portion of daily life in everything from harvesting and sourcing food to the undertaking of healing rituals and rites of passage, of which priestesses played such a significant role.

The first calendars were based entirely on the moon cycle of 29.5 days, with twelve cycles equating to one year. It is believed that the Sumerians were the first to develop the lunar calendar and from their initial work the Babylonian, Ancient Greek, Roman, Egyptian and Hebrew calendars were heavily influenced.[2] Moon worship, rituals and practices can be found in many ancient societies including the Celts and Egyptians, and the moon is acknowledged as a powerful life and spiritual force in many practices such as astrology, Ayurveda and Taoism, as well as indigenous cultures throughout the world.

The moon has always been deeply associated with women and seen as a symbol of powerful fertility, especially as the moon cycle closely mirrors the menstrual cycle. The word 'moon' originates from the word *menses* meaning month or moon, which is now, of course, what we know as the time of menstruation.[3] *Menses* morphed into the Proto-Germanic word *menon*, then the Old English word *mona* to the Middle English word *mone*, all of which mean moon.[4] The Latin word *mensis* also means month, which in turn relates to the ancient Greek word for moon, *mene*.[5] The powerful ancient Greek goddess of the moon and the passage of time, Selene, was also known as 'Mene'.

The moon circles around the earth in 29.5 days in a complete cycle. The cycle begins with the new moon when the moon is completely dark and not visible, and it then grows in shape until it reaches its peak at the full moon, going back to the dark of the new moon every cycle. Each phase of the cycle presents us with a particular opportunity to work with lunar energies which help us to powerfully connect with the moon and ourselves in ways that can enhance our life, spiritual practice and power as a priestess.

Committing to charting the moon cycles and your own emotions, energies and actions with it is an incredibly powerful thing to do as a priestess. Add in the charting of your menstrual cycle as well, and you have a potent personal practice that can help you to tap into both cosmic and personal energies that can support you to know yourself at a deeper and more powerful level. If you find yourself particularly aligned with the moon's energies, or simply commit to becoming so, it can also help you better understand your thoughts and behaviours at times of the lunar cycle, especially if they have you feeling confused or even upset at not knowing what may be fully happening to or for you.

All my life I have experienced a change in my sleep at the time of the full moon. I just never knew that was what it was related to until I learned more about how the moon's cycle was a reflection of my own. At first, I called it a disturbance. Now I know better! Most of the time I sleep soundly, but at the time of the full moon and its bringing of restlessness, illumination, brightness and energy, I often wake as early as 3.30 a.m. to 4.30 a.m. and rarely can get back to sleep.

This bothered me enormously for a long time and I would often get frustrated with myself when it was happening. Why it took me so long to recognise a pattern was repeating itself so regularly one can only ask of the Goddess! Once I started to track my thoughts, feelings, behaviours and menstrual cycle with the lunar cycle, it became evident that my early morning waking only ever occurred at the time of the full moon and that I was simply being stirred into action, even if it was dark outside and many hours away from sunrise.

And as soon as I stopped resisting this and trying to force myself back to sleep, but rather embracing it and rising to be in prayer, at my altar, making plans, or writing this book, I found so many other areas of my life began to flow. Much of this book has been written in the seeming dead of night, but in fact has been a time of potent shining under the light of the full moon.

How can the moon and following its power, energy and cycles help you to create an even more powerful spiritual way of being for you as a priestess?

**Let's find out.**

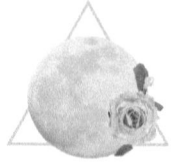

# Living Illuminated

The lunar phases of the moon present a beautiful opportunity for you as a spiritual leader to tap into their power as a reflection of your own. Cycling and working with the lunar phases, and feeling into the potency of their different gifts, can see you truly experience deep and 'proper' rest when you need it most, rather than just a surface nap or quick pause in your day. And it can help you align to when is a magical time for you to be in action, riding a wave of light, momentum and energy so that you can amplify everything you wish to create and bring to life.

The following are brief descriptions of the lunar phases and how you can work with each of them.

### New Moon

The moon at this phase is not visible. This is a time of the shadow, our subconscious mind and inner world. It is a great time for inner work, reflection, and leaning into the lessons of your shadow, as well as slowing down, resting and self-care.

### Waxing Crescent Moon

The moon at this phase starts to slowly come in to light and be visible again. This is a wonderful time to set intentions for something you wish to manifest and attract. Take what you are desiring from your head and heart and make it known by writing it down and speaking it aloud.

### First Quarter Moon

The moon at this phase is now half lit. This is a time for you to feel into what you truly need for your intention to grow, strengthen and come to life. Make a list. Draw up a plan. Step out the actions required for you to create the reality you are desiring. This is a time of rising energy that you can ride the wave of.

### Waxing Gibbous Moon

The moon at this phase is almost full and is inviting you to move fully ahead with your plans for your intention. It's time for you to step into the light and your highest good. Reach out to others, seek support and get organised, so that you have strong foundations to keep springboarding into action.

### Full Moon

The moon at this phase is lusciously bright and full. This is a time of expansion, abundance and growth. The full moon can bring you feelings of energy and also sometimes vivid dreams and restless sleep. Your emotions can be high. This is a great time to create, socialise and be in your full power.

### Waning Gibbous Moon

The moon at this phase represents the ending of expansion. Your positive work is now ripening and requires tending to, but also the waning moon as it softens its light invites you to begin reflecting and releasing any blocks that may be impeding you. This is so you can fully harvest the rewards of the work you have done.

### Last Quarter Moon

The moon at this phase is moving towards a dark phase again. This is the time to fully harvest your intentions and actions, evaluate how far you have come and what you have been able to reap. What were you able to bring to life and what can you learn for the next cycle?

### Waning Crescent Moon

The moon at this phase is a small crescent and you may now experience a dip in your energy levels calling you to rest and be in gratitude for all the moon has given you this cycle. It is time to feel into the gentle power of restoration as a new moon cycle is about to begin.

The great beauty of the lunar cycle is that every month you are presented with a divine opportunity to connect with its energy and how it can support you in the life you want to lead as a priestess.

The lunar cycle can support you as you dream, set intentions, make plans, step into power and action, harvest and reflect and give thanks, all while shining your full light and honouring your needs for self-care, rest and restoration. This in turn means you can experience greater energy, understanding of your body, abundance, joy and success, and less stress, confusion and disconnection from yourself while the moon acts as a source of illumination, flow, cycling, rebirth and regeneration for you.

And all the time this is happening you are flowing and reconnecting over and over again with the cosmic power of this heavenly body which will only magnify your own beauty and power as a spiritual being. And as you do so do not be surprised if you inspire those around you to become fascinated with *La Luna* as well.

> Even Glenn now says, *'Ooh* ... beautiful bright full moon tonight. I wonder what time you will wake us up!'

# A Bleeding Shame

How did you first learn about menarche? Did your mum, dad or a trusted adult tell you openly and without hesitation what may occur for you, or for someone that you knew? Because, let's face it, it's not only young girls, women or transgender folk who menstruate who can benefit greatly from understanding what the menstrual cycle is! Were you maybe not told at all and had to find out yourself? Or told hurriedly and with embarrassment? And did anyone tell you that menstruation was a spiritual practice that was a beautiful and powerful experience?

No.

Well, hold on to your menstrual cup or cloth pad ... a significant part of your life might be about to change for the better!

The experience of learning about a first period for many of us is filled with uncomfortableness and confusion. This is more often than not due to menstrual shame, which is a very real phenomenon, even if we don't realise we have been touched by it. Menstrual shame has been with us for thousands of years. The power of the Blood Mysteries, which involve menarche, birth and menopause, have become buried under a tidal wave of patriarchal dominance, medicalisation and capitalism. But they are being reclaimed and priestesses as spiritual leaders are leading the way in them being so.

A long time before it was known that human conception required fertilisation, women were thought to generate new life simply by withholding their menstrual blood when they chose to, and menopause was not seen as something that was a sign of loss. Rather it was viewed as a time of increased power for older women as they chose to retain their blood as the source of creation nearer to the end of their life. A woman was powerful. And a bleeding woman even more so.[6]

In some traditional societies, menstrual rituals were incredibly empowering and allowed women to come together in ways that honoured their bleeding self, giving them space and time to rest and feel deeply into their bleeding time. The women of the Kalasha Valley in Pakistan came together in communion in a large menstrual house known as a *bashali*. This was considered a holy place and deeply respected by men.[7] In some ancient cultures a menstruating woman was considered to not only be sacred and powerful but even psychic, and the Native American Cherokee people believed that menstrual blood was a source of strength and that it could be used for both healing and destructive purposes.[8]

The spread of Christianity and other patriarchal religions saw the rise of menstrual shame, and menarche, childbirth and menopause were recast. And women's bodies along with them. The womb and menstrual bleeding were no longer seen to be a source of creation and power. Body and spirit were torn apart with an ever increasing medical model making it even more so. Menstrual taboos became the norm and feelings of shame, embarrassment and fear came with them. In some societies and religions, menstruation, menstrual blood and simply women themselves, both during their time of menstruation and non-menstruation, came to be seen as unclean, dirty and even dangerous. The bleeding woman was seen to be in need of hiding and what was taking place with her body was not to be discussed in any way.

And while we may think that things are a great deal better—and in many ways they are—strong evidence of menstrual shame still exists today. We are bombarded with messages that the 'crazy' symptoms of premenstrual syndrome (PMS) require medication, all babies are endangered if they are not born in a hospital with medical intervention, periods are an inconvenience or even a 'curse' and menopausal symptoms should be shunted away. We don't even seem to be able to acknowledge what our blood actually looks like when we see sanitary products advertised with blue liquid. Menstrual blood is red. Red not blue! Now that's shame in action.

And in turn the result of this is that the power and beauty of the Blood Mysteries remain distant to many of us rather than something that can be claimed, honoured and seen as a spiritual practice of great beauty and power. We have come a way, but we still have a way to go.

If you are at a stage in your life where you are menstruating and you are yet to find and feel into the incredible power of your bleeding self, then the time is nigh for you as a priestess to do so. The intense and beautiful spiritual power it will add to your life cannot be underestimated and it will also change the way you see childbirth, whether you actually give birth to a child or not, and menopause for yourself or others as well.

# Your Blood is Beautiful

The Blood Mysteries bring great change to our lives in not just physical ways, but ways that are emotionally and spiritually profound as well. We can experience deeper wisdom and physical connection to ourselves and others through these experiences and a reclaiming, or honouring for the first time, of the great power we hold within our bodies.

Menstrual and birthing blood is holy and healing. It creates and nurtures life and places those who bleed as central to the power of creation. Reclaiming your bleeding self is an act that is both ancient, and also radically new, in a modern world that still teaches us that we should not discuss periods openly, let alone that they can be a profoundly spiritual practice.

In the cycle of menstruation, the time of bleeding is one of great personal and spiritual power. It is not unusual for bleeding to bring forth spiritual gifts such as deeper intuition, psychic visions, a deeper sense of oneness with the Great Mother, communication with spirits, heightened senses, and the receiving of powerful soul downloads. Bleeding time is magical, as is the entire menstrual cycle, however if you are not attuned to it, it will be unlikely you experience such things, or if you do experience them, you dismiss them through lack of understanding.

The menstrual cycle is one more powerful way that we can see ourselves as extraordinary beings who are constantly in a cycling state of birth/creation, life/harvesting, death/ending and rebirth/renewal. And that our inner world is a deep and divine reflection of the lunar cycle and seasonal cycles of the Great Mother as well. Our menstrual blood binds these divine cycles together over and over again presenting to us a powerful spiritual practice and way of being that can support us to feel more connected to our bodies, personal power, the earth, the moon and each other.

Learning to love your bleeding self is a powerful act of reclamation and there are multiple ways you can do so to enhance your life and spiritual self as a priestess.

# Bloody Rites

If you are menstruating, the following will be of particular interest to you. If you have never menstruated, or are no longer, I encourage you to see how closely (and beautifully) the spiritual practice of menstruation mirrors that of the moon, and in a yearly cycle the earth's seasons, making it something that we can all access and be a part of, regardless of whether we are menstruating or not.

Each menstrual cycle presents a divinely spiritual opportunity to understand our bodies better and pay attention to any healing and releasing we are called to. Tapping into the spiritual power of menstruation does not require special skills, simply a willingness to be present with the varying phases of our menstrual cycle. Paying attention to it each time it comes around and not ignoring it, is where one starts.

If you begin to regularly observe the moon and work with lunar magic, you will often note that your menstrual cycle will begin to align with its phases as well. You may, as in ancient times, ovulate with the full moon and bleed at the new moon, or the opposite. Or your cycle may show itself to you in many other ways as well. There is no right or wrong way here.

The menstrual cycle is also divided into four quarters like the earth's seasons. Each week of the cycle is divinely aligned with the Great Mother's seasons in a myriad of ways, presenting opportunities to us for a beautiful and very personal spiritual practice. Each phase we can come to see, feel and understand how our energy, attitude and embodiment is different and how they align to the cycles around us. This is not to say that everything is going to be magically aligned in every way! And it certainly won't feel that way if you don't commit to paying attention to it. However, if you do pay attention, you will soon learn how deeply aligned your body and inner world can be with the outer world around you. And the outcome? A divinely held and known sense of connection to yourself and the earth and energies around you.

If you educate yourself on where you are in your menstrual cycle, at any time, you can learn to follow and go with your own life flow with more grace and ease. Here is some more information about how you can approach and learn from the energies of the varying times in your menstrual cycle.

## Week One
**(Days 1 to 7)**

*Themes: Death Rebirth Ending - Season: Late winter to early spring - Moon phase: New moon.*

The time where you are bleeding is one of quiet and stillness. It is a powerful time to let go of anything that no longer serves you including habits, thoughts, beliefs and patterns. Honour yourself by retreating from the busyness of your life in small ways by doing things such as taking a nap, having a ritual bath or curling up in a quiet corner with a book. This is a time that calls for your gentleness, kindness and compassion and when your bleeding finishes, you can take the wisdom and reflections you have gleaned to positively and powerfully influence your next phase. As that next phase nears and the feelings connected to early spring rise, it is a good time to write and express your intentions on what you wish to achieve next.

## Week Two
**(Days 8 to 14):**

*Themes: Energy Creativity Birthing - Season: Late spring to early summer - Moon phase: Waxing.*

Your cycle builds to a peak at this time of ovulation where you will likely experience an increase in your physical, emotional, sexual and creative energy. Your desire to create and bring to life projects will be high and you may have a desire to be more social, host people at your home and go to events. This is a great time to bring to life something that is tugging at your heart or a project in your business or career, not to mention those intentions you set in your previous phase. This phase of your cycle is also the perfect time to be sensual and embodied through sex, dancing, exercise and anything else that gets your heart racing and blood pumping!

## Week Three
**(Days 15 to 21):**

*Themes: Gratitude Harvesting Slowing Down - Season: Late summer to early autumn - Moon phase: Full.*

You are now post-ovulation and this can be a time of mixed

feelings, often dependent upon whether you were able to achieve what you intended during your creative and energetic peak. You will likely have strong feelings of wanting to rid yourself of unnecessary things and confront things that are not working for you in the way you want them to. You are calling yourself to your own attention so that you can learn and not repeat any patterns in your next cycle that have not served you in this one. This is also a time of celebration and gentle joy as you honour what you have achieved—no matter how big or small—in this phase. And potent energy will be within and surrounding you not to start a new project, but rather to finish any off that require loose ends to be knotted, rubber stamps to be given, submissions to be made and things to be closed off.

## Week Four
**(Days 22 to 28):**

*Themes: Power Clarity Purpose - Season: Late autumn to early winter - Moon phase: Waning.*

You will now be presented with lessons from your menstrual cycle to both see and feel into for your own spiritual learning and guidance. You may feel powerful and glad for where you have arrived or frustrated that an old pattern has shown itself to you again. Either way there is medicine for you to lean into and learn from. This is a powerful time of surrendering to your bleeding phase which is soon to come and with it your darker inner winter. Any preparations you do for yourself as that time approaches such as clearing your calendar, making a nourishing pot of soup or ensuring you have more rest time ahead, will serve you deeply. As you begin to slow down and gain clarity on how you want the next phase of your cycle to show it yourself to you, you may feel a growing desire to be less available to others and more to yourself as you honour the bleeding phase that is to come.

The menstrual cycle is a divine alchemical process of great power, transformation and wisdom. The more we choose to honour and understand it the more we acknowledge and can come to love and respect all parts of ourselves. This is particularly potent for a practice that has for so long been shrouded in shame and secrecy, disavowed for its true power and spiritual nature, including its connection to the lunar and earth cycles.

This makes the reclaiming of our menstrual powers to be one that is not just individual in nature, but also one that collectively heals sisterhood, and any woman that has felt suppressed and ashamed of her bleeding self before our time and around us now.

# It's Inevitable

**Change, that is. It's inevitable in our lives and touches us all.**

Nothing stays the same or is static, especially when as spiritual beings, we are reflected in the beauty of the changing cycles of life around us.

I am sure that, like me, there have been times in your life where you have not wanted things to change. The comfort, or sometimes even discomfort, of where we are can feel safer and less scary than what may lie ahead. And this is one of the reasons—our fear of or resistance to change—that can see us hold times of life transition at arms-length.

I have often wondered if part of the reason we resist change and want the status quo to remain, is because we don't honour and celebrate change and transitions in the way we truly can, embracing them for how they are a part of the cycle of life. Would we cope better with change if we honoured the transitions we were going through with more reverence, spirit and love? Even if they were murky, confusing or hard? I think we would. And in doing so it would open up divine portals for us to more deeply understand ourselves and the true magic of our human and lived existence.

In the fast-paced modern world in which we live, change is a constant. It is extremely rare for us to have one job or career our entire lives. And with that comes change, transition, starting over and new learning. We may have a number of significant intimate relationships in our lifetime, unlike our ancestors who may have had just one. And with that comes grief, letting go, lessons and new ways of loving. We may have more than one spiritual awakening or period of deep exploration in our time here on earth. And with that comes newness, darkness, fear, alchemy, pain and joy.

And sometimes we don't even realise we are undergoing deep change or changes, or if we do, we push them down or ignore them, hoping they may go away. They never do. Because inevitable, right? Right. It's those spaces in between in our lives that we think are nothing, but in fact are so important and often where divine alchemical shifts, upgrades, releases and openings are occurring. We often don't see them in this way because they come with uncomfortableness, restlessness, and a feeling of being in a void or like nothing is happening. We may be in a void, but something is still happening! It is a space where we are changing, shifting, growing and getting ready for the next iteration of our life and being.

Whenever you notice yourself becoming fearful or resistant to change, one of the most powerful things you can do for yourself is to get curious. Know that you are having a very normal reaction to shifting into something new, but don't let that stop you or keep you stagnant. Eventually you will get swept along with the change that will occur whether you want to or not. Therefore, would it not be best to embrace the adventure that comes with it or make a commitment to being a clear vessel of what is to come? Who knows what lies ahead! It could be better and more beautiful than you ever could imagine.

The changes you are going through in life, at any time or stage, are a divine reflection of your connection to the Great Mother, the moon, the sun, the seasons, your menstrual cycle if you experience one, and simply life in general. You are a cyclic being that will sometimes whirl and spin with incredible power. You are also a cyclic being that will sometimes gently wind and unwind with softness and tenderness. And every change you go through from your maiden/young years to your mother/creator years to your maga/wise years to your crone/old years becomes one that you can embrace with your whole heart if you choose to.

And a priestess always chooses herself, knowing that the journey she is going on is one that is divinely laid out for her and meant to be taken. And that just like the Great Mother, change, ageing, cycling, birth, rebirth, death—and so much more—waits for no one. The pulse of life around us reflects that which runs through our own body, making change a beautiful constant we can try to ignore or fully embrace.

JULIE PARKER

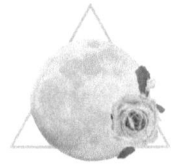

# Death Becomes You

---

As a priestess, learning to embrace the full spectrum of life is a part of your calling. And that calling includes the embracing of death.

Up until barely 100 years ago, life and death were a co-joined part of daily existence. Industrialisation in the nineteenth century saw us surrounded by infant mortality, battlefield slayings and untreatable illnesses. Most people lived only to middle age or younger. With medical advancements, better safety procedures, education and technology, we now live longer. Death is therefore further away for us and often not a usual part of our daily lives. We have pushed it to the edges of our existence as something that will happen 'one day.'

It is much easier, as well as more socially acceptable, to only focus on life and living in our daily lives, but this does not give us the full picture of what it means to be a cyclic being. The cycle of life shows us that every living thing eventually decays, descends and dies, or simply dies. Everything. And while it is understandable to be focused on living fully, denial of death harms us all. And is a potent form of spiritual bypassing.

Death has so much to teach us, even through heart-ripping pain and grief. I have been there and will be again. I am sure you have and know you will be again too. This is not easy. Our shadow and the parts of us that experience fear and the deepest transformation never are. However, do we really wish to hold death at arm's length through measures such as meticulously counting calories, exercising until exhaustion, trying to 'reverse' ageing, isolating the sick and dying away from us while we try to sanitise our minds of anything related to death? Is that really living?

Much of the embracing of death is about surrendering to its inevitability, which is not about giving up or somehow not living to our fullest. It is about making peace with what is and choosing to embrace both life and death as they show up for us. And our ability or inability to surrender in this way, is undoubtedly related to the level of peace and contentment we experience in our lives and how connected we are spiritually to our own vastness.

I believe death is about transformation. By embracing, or at least acknowledging death in a more accepting way, we place ourselves in a powerful container of transformation. We are given opportunities on a daily basis to transform and see what does not serve us. And death can occur in many ways, not just when someone or something dies. Death can be the end of a personal identity, a dream, a job, a relationship. And there can be infinite opportunities within these deaths if we are open to seeing them. They can be used as a catalyst to propel us into living and loving to a much fuller extent and all of them can lead to transformation and the opening of a portal for rebirth for us.

As a priestess you can be a powerful living example and catalyst for death by doing challenging but also simple things such as talking about it with loved ones, not hiding it from children and openly discussing your own end of life and how you want that to be embraced and celebrated. Doing so sees you know death not as the opposite of life, but as part of it.

When we say yes to death, we say yes to life.
We are choosing to embrace it all.
And in doing so embrace all of ourselves as well.

# Celebrating You

Celebrating yourself is a part of your spiritual connection to both the cycles and beauty of life.

And you are so worthy of celebrating.

What you bring to the world, simply by your presence, is a gift that no one else has or can bring forth. And in all your joy, frailties, fire, love and commitment to this life there is much to celebrate in that.

While we may be used to celebrating our birthdays, or a major occasion like a wedding or birth, so often it is the 'smaller' and seemingly less significant moments of our lives we don't deem worthy of marking. It may also be that we simply don't know how powerful and significant they are, or that we have been 'denied' them as a result of patriarchal oppression. There are so many rites of passage, transitions and experiences in our lives that carry such deep significance for us as cyclical and spiritual beings that are worth celebrating in a myriad of ways.

Celebrating something for ourselves is about distinguishing it from the everyday happenings of life, and making something special and reverent out of it. It's about taking and making meaning of something because you choose to. For you. If you look for ways to celebrate yourself and changes, transitions and significant happenings in your life, you will find them everywhere, especially those that are physical, emotional and spiritual in nature that you may not have been aware of in the patriarchal landscape in which we live. It's time to reclaim them. And create more.

Some of us may have grown up in a culture or religion where certain rites of passage such as menarche or puberty were celebrated beautifully. Lucky you if that was your experience! If it has not been so, however, then know that no matter how old you are or what your cultural background or spiritual beliefs, there are a myriad of beautiful ways you can honour and celebrate yourself at times throughout your life. There is no time like the present to begin celebrating and honouring yourself in deeper ways, and making room and time to do so is important as a priestess. It is a way to stop, pause, honour yourself and give deep gratitude for who you are and how your life is unfolding, or what you want to change and have unfold in a different way. Celebrating yourself is a divine way to get in touch with who you are at any given moment.

Changes in our bodies are a call that we are undergoing a major life transition and those are always worth celebrating. Menarche, pregnancy, birth and menopause are significant life experiences and while we will likely be very excited about a wanted pregnancy and the arrival of a new soul, menarche and menopause are still so often shrouded in secrecy and shame and not celebrated at all.

There are then so many other firsts in our life such as the first time we went to school, kissed someone, had sex, drove a car or got a job.

There are also emotional and spiritual experiences in our lives such as the first time we stood up for ourselves, ended a relationship that was not serving us, put ourselves first, took a huge leap of faith, did something that terrified us, travelled solo, paid for something significant with money we earned or did something that was really hard but had to be done.

And the ways in which you can celebrate yourself are infinite. A ceremonial walk, hike or moonlit swim when you enter menopause. A party or gathering when you get a new job or retire. The crafting or making of a keepsake when you took a big risk or entirely changed yourself with courage and conviction. A cleansing or releasing ritual if you get divorced, end something, or let something or someone go.

The core and most important thing is to celebrate yourself and the special transitions and moments in your life like you matter. Because you do. Every part of you.

To honour and acknowledge yourself in this way opens up gateways for you to see and step into new phases of your life in a conscious way. It's the antithesis of just letting things pass by and not making something special out of them. It's about making something special out of them. Because you are special and deserve to show yourself that as often as possible.

Life is a divine experience to be cherished and savoured in every moment possible. Celebrating yourself and the major changes, transitions, learnings and rites of passage you go through is one way of bringing forth that savouring in a way that honours you for the divine soul and priestess you are.

# You're a Wild One

We are terribly civil as women on the whole. So courteous and polite. And while courtesy and politeness have their place, they can also contribute to us being over-domesticated, over-socialised, non-boundaried and people-pleasers. All of which contribute to the loss of our inherent wild nature.

In the time of the ancient priestess women were very individualised. They did not exist for male pleasure or gaze, or simply to assist, counsel or mother them. Women's natural instincts and ability to be free were fully known to them, unlike it is today in our patriarchal world, which conditions girls and even babies to hide their true selves. We constantly tell little girls not to cry, be angry or upset, and focus on them needing to be 'nice' and in many instances decorative too.

The path and embodiment of the wild woman is therefore unknown to so many if not all of us. Being wild and fully free is not seen as acceptable for women by mainstream society and therefore exploring this side of ourselves is taking a step into the unknown. And with that unknown and loss of control we often experience fear and a sense of danger, neither of which are inherently bad, but can make us reconsider if our wild woman is worth exploring. She always is.

Whatever our own wildness may be is not written or structured, just like the Great Mother herself. It is a deep-seated feeling within our body, the intuitive call of our soul voice, and the primal rawness of our own instincts where we are in touch with our own rhythm and cycles. The wild within is our untameable animal nature that represents our full soul's essence and is vital for our spiritual wellbeing, exploration and sovereignty as a priestess. Harnessing the power of our wild woman essence can lead us into greater action and evolved thinking. She is also the part of us that is unashamed, a rebel and a revolutionary, something which is deeply threatening to the patriarchy. If women rose up together, unashamed and unafraid of who they truly are and their own instinctual power, the world order would change.

A wild woman lives inside all of us and at one point in time or another you have likely felt Her, even if just for a moment. She may have come forth after loving and extended time spent with the Great Mother, in a deep personal yoga practice, at an ecstatic dance party, while having sex, or speaking passionately about something that is important to you. In these moments, we release any ancient fears of rejection and disconnection we may carry and even if just for a short time, we remember our wild again. And if we can do it for that period of time, we can do it for more.

Whatever your wild woman calls you to do know that ignoring Her comes at your own peril. She is the whisper or roar, that rises in you when you feel bound and unable to fully express yourself spiritually, emotionally, physically or sexually. She is the part of you that wants you to leave that soul sucking job, release yourself of the societal or familial expectations of getting married and becoming a mother, be wildly creative, dress the way you truly want to and wholly own your sexuality and sexual desires as an extension of your true self. She wants you to be free and in whatever way is possible for you—live with passion, desire, intent and purpose—abandoning societal and patriarchal expectations that do not serve you.

Her deep spiritual calling is for you to ask yourself and then act upon these questions: 'What do I want for myself and my life?' and 'How can I be free?'

# Sister Healing

I once knew a woman who said she did not trust other women and that she would rather be friends with and in the company of men. My relationship with her changed from that moment, as ironically her lack of trust in me as a woman made me trust her less. I did not feel safe with her knowing she felt this way, or that I was able to fully be myself. Her believing that I was somehow the enemy expected to strike at her made me hyper-vigilant about being around her. And while I did not blame her for feeling this way, our relationship ended because I felt increasingly uncertain about what she expected or wanted of me.

Many of us have sister wounds of this kind as a result of things such as bullying, exclusion and betrayal. And they have been particularly present amongst us since the onset of the patriarchy, which ripped us apart as women who once relied so heavily on each other in close-knit communities.

I don't profess to know what women's relationships were like before the patriarchy. None of us can. One can only imagine what they would have been like. However, in a world where women were seen as sacred and powerful, not weak or to be mistrusted, it feels relatively safe to assume that there was a level of connection and community that was at the forefront of women's relationships, rather than the somewhat competitive and comparison-laced environments we can now find ourselves in.

A sister wound can present itself to you in many ways, some of which you may not even be aware of. Hello shadow! It may show up in feelings of mistrust, worry or suspicion about women around you, those that you know or don't, and behaviours such as jealousy, comparison and judgement. It can see you do things such as holding back from being vulnerable with women especially about things you are struggling with, not wanting to work with them in teams, partnerships or projects, sometimes with no real understanding why, avoiding being a part of women's groups or gatherings, projecting your suspicion or fear onto them, or simply avoiding women altogether. And if you do have any of these feelings, or behave in these ways, it of course does not make you a bad person. It simply means you are human, and like us all, traversing life in the best way you can.

Committing to healing your sister wounds can profoundly change your life, not just in your relationships with women but in relationship with yourself as well. And as you are now aware, anything that transforms your relationship with yourself, especially as a priestess, is so worthwhile undertaking.

In opening up a gateway for you to heal any sister wounds you may have, know that I am not suggesting you need to have a connected and loving relationship with all women. That is not realistic and could in fact be detrimental to you. It certainly would be for me. We all know of people that are simply not for us. A boundary we have needed to set or fundamental differences in values can make it clear someone is not meant to be in our lives. This is powerful discernment and important to exercise when it comes to consciously choosing who we spend time with.

I think you likely know the sort of thoughts, feelings and behaviours in relation to women I am talking about. If you have recognised yourself in these words and experiences, then this wound exists for you, and only you can heal it. And along that path if you are radically honest and take full self-responsibility, you may recognise that you have done things such as judged, excluded or betrayed other women, even as you have experienced them yourself. Therefore, the healing required here may be multi-layered and involve forgiveness, reflection, releasing, shifting thoughts and more forgiveness—of yourself—again.

Your intuition and inner wisdom will guide you on how best to tend your sister wounds and become a stronger, more powerful and connected priestess as a result. It may look like healing conversations, working in deeper collaboration with women, reaching out even when scared, and committing to meeting new women and forging new beginnings. What is most important is the healing that you undergo as you do so and how that will gently and compassionately change how you show up for yourself and other women moving forward.

And the healing that you do so reverently for yourself here not only mends your heart but does so for the collective sisterhood as well. One more healed and healing woman equals untold numbers of other healed and healing women, rising not alone and separate, but together, in powerful and sacred leadership that will change the world.

# Being In Body

If you are anything like me, you're a bit of an overthinker. Well, okay. Maybe more than a bit.

So many of us are in our heads and living a great deal in the top section of our bodies. We think so regularly about things, like what we should do next, how something may impact others, if we are doing it right, if it is enough, if we are enough. It's a lot to traverse, and in many ways, if we are not conscious of our ego and thoughts in compassionate ways, the more we think about such things, the more we can remain almost entirely in a thinking state.

For us to truly be able to get out of our thinking mind and into the full spectrum of all other parts of ourselves, we have to get in greater touch with our bodies. When we are living in a highly cerebral way it can be easy to forget how powerful our bodies are in our lives and spiritual journeys. We take them for granted and not just in relation to our health. Being truly *in* our bodies opens up an entire world of spiritual connection and possibilities for us that our brains and thinking state never can. It's where we can become truly grounded, powerful, sexual, driven and electric, entirely owning our physical and personal power.

Agency over our bodies has been diminished for women by patriarchal and religious oppression, all with the intent to try and disconnect us from the power of our embodied selves. This includes things such as menstruation, masturbation, sex and sexual expression being labelled as shameful, and even that we are too delicate to exercise. Heaven forbid we should sweat, puff or get flushed in the face and feel the power of being fully energised and alive from movement! Women are too powerful and too dangerous to the suppressive status quo when we are fully in our bodies in these ways, and so the reclaiming of our own personal space and bodies makes it not just individually potent, but collectively so as well.

Committing to truly connecting with and being more in your own body has infinite benefits for you as a priestess. It allows you to know more deeply the signs and signals of your own body when you are feeling heightened emotions or have needs. It supports you to connect to your soul voice and intuition at a deeper level where you have more ability to feel into your gut, heart and womb space. It allows you to be more expressive emotionally, physically, spiritually, sexually and creatively. And it ignites within you your personal power from deep within your body, honouring it as the living temple you walk through life in every day. This makes embodiment and truly being in sovereign ownership of your body about coming into your whole self and not seeing yourself as separate or compartmentalised in any way.

A wonderful place to start with becoming more embodied is with your breath. If you hold your breath or consistently breathe in a shallow way, you interrupt your own life force, which can make your body feel stiff and painful. By paying loving attention to your breath through practices such as deep breathing, breathwork and gently reminding yourself to slow down and breathe more deeply into the full base of your lungs, you become more strongly present with yourself and everything your body is communicating to you. And if you are a meditator, you will clearly know the incredible ally that deep and powerful breathing is to opening up your spiritual awareness and connection to yourself in any given moment.

From the world of our inner breath, deep embodiment becomes all about movement, and specifically to support you to truly get back in your body and feel the immense power you have as a spiritual being and priestess, movement that helps you to feel joyful, alive, and connected to the Great Mother and others around you. This will likely see you get breathing (consciously), dancing, touching, loving and making love, rolling, stretching and running wild in ways that feel fun and fabulous to you. As women we are collectively calling ourselves to dance, play, skip, have sex, lay on the earth and do something—anything—that helps us feel electrically energised and more deeply connected to our own life force. And if it's been a while, or even never, since you felt embodied in this way, you will amaze yourself at how aligned and empowered you will feel to yourself and how much your spiritual awareness and connection will open as a result.

Your beautiful body is calling you to listen and pay loving attention to it and then move, in any way that supports you to feel free, unencumbered and powerful. To develop for yourself a delicious space of feeling both wonderful free, abandoned and out of control and simultaneously *in* control as well.

Once you find what truly works for you and helps you get right back into the power of your own body, don't ever stop. Keep going.

**In fact, dance on forever. And then some more.**

# Anam Cara

My journey as a priestess has just begun. There is so much more to explore and for that I am profoundly grateful. I hope if this path is opening up for you, it is just the beginning of more for you too.

One of the things I am most excited about is moving deeper into the spiritual practices of my Celtic ancestors. There is a whole world waiting for me that my first ancestral trip to England, Scotland and Ireland recently has simply whetted my appetite for.

And as it is with any significant journey in life so often what we go looking for is not all we find. I expected to love the land of where my lineage comes from but not nearly as much as I did. The wilderness, lochs and wildflowers of Scotland lit up every cell in my body. The rolling green hills of Ireland filled me with a sense of magic and wonder I had not felt since I was a girl. And the deeply divine feminine power of Avalon had me bone deep knowing a sense of earthly belonging I will carry with me forever. And as I journey on this path, I have come to learn that I must maintain a strong commitment to being my own greatest guide above all else and a wayshower for all I need to know and keep gently moving towards.

There is a Celtic expression *anam cara*, which means 'soul friend', popularised by Irish philosopher John O'Donohue in his beautiful book of the same name.⁹ In the Celtic tradition a soul friend was someone who was considered to be an integral part of your spiritual development, a beloved person, guide and confidant who was there for you at times of need and growth with compassion, love and presence. And so, to me, an anam cara is undoubtedly a priestess in all Her forms.

What has struck me about the true beauty of anam cara is how as priestesses as we gently unfold our lives, is how vital we be our own soul guide—our own anam cara—and to live as a priestess every day is to know there is no one path or way. Only your way.

May you be open and willing to all that your anam cara has for you on your priestess path.

She knows you like no other and is calling you into your own life version of beauty, grace and spiritual service as the priestess you are right now. And will continue to be called to be.

# PART VI

# Your Priestess Gifts

You have sacred gifts. We all do. You may know them, or they may be still revealing themselves to you. So often our sacred gifts are the things we take for granted about ourselves; what comes naturally to us with ease and grace that we barely notice. Often our gifts are what we are praised and thanked for and what we can hold well and share generously.

As a priestess, one of my most significant sacred gifts is that of a clarifier and initiator. I am a sword wielder and have a way of getting to the heart of things quickly, helping someone make sense of what is unfolding for them to sit more deeply where they are or move beyond. This comes forth in me as a counsellor, a coach, a sacred circle holder and a speaker. Almost always it is connected to the quality of questions I ask someone and the unconditional love and regard in which I hold them as I do. This is the Cerridwen and Dark Goddesses of transformation that live within me.

Another one of my sacred gifts as a priestess is as a beautifier. Creating divine spaces for people to gather is incredibly important to me and something I take with more than a pinch of seriousness. The flowers, the candles, the scents and the atmosphere of a space I create, I consider to be vital to the experience that a soul is about to have in my company. I adore ensuring that everything has its place and is set with the most loving and divine intention. This is something that will take me hours in a meditative and giving state if I can take the time and it supports the intention I have for every person that is going to be present with me. This is the Aphrodite, Freyja and Love Goddesses of beauty that live within me.

Your sacred gifts as a priestess are with you this very moment. They always have been. They are a part of your soul blueprint, handed down to you through generations of love, culture, tears, practice, and embodiment, and of course, can be cultivated by you further or as something that is newly unfolding to you now. You get to claim and work with them as a modern spiritual leader, using them to continually heal yourself and us all as a collective as you do.

Let's learn more about some of the magic and gifts that you as a priestess may have within you or are about to be inspired by and bring forth. May you always be inspired to bring them into service in significant and meaningful ways for yourself and others.

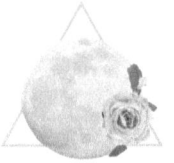

# The Ritual Priestess

You love the slow, intuitive power of ritual, a prayer in motion that honours the sacred, helping us to move into a physical and energetic state for what we are about to undertake or complete. You believe that rituals are carriers of deep meaning and make our lives richer and more divine.

As a priestess who loves to participate in and conduct rituals you know that everything—yes, everything—we do in life has meaning. And can have a deeper meaning if we desire it to. A bath, cooking, gardening, journalling, all present to you as experiences that can be enhanced by ritual.

You are deeply intuitive and trust the magic of how things unfold in these moments, knowing that expensive tools are not required for you to design and execute beautiful experiences. In saying that you do love the process of carefully choosing things such as music, herbs, cloths, statues, crystals or essential oil sprays to support what you wish to bring to life!

When you create ritual space and perform rituals as a priestess you become a vessel of empty presence and a sword like reflection of truth, where you, and those you are in service to, can be felt, seen and understood at the deepest levels. You create rituals that are touching, moving and divine, helping stir something within people so that they may connect to the lower, middle and upper realms for their highest good.

Creating atmosphere, connection and wonder is a part of your magical skill set as you undertake things such as opening a sacred circle, honouring a moon phase, connecting people in group meditation or opening a space. You can reverently invite in all spirits, elements and supportive powers to your space as your allies, at times that help people mark important and honoured occasions in their life, or simply because you and they desire to infuse an experience with more sacredness.

People look up to you as a deep holder of space and igniter of reverence and spirit. Which you are. You make every occasion and gathering more beautiful and your own life more so in your personal rituals as well.

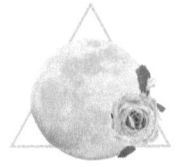

# The Ceremonial Priestess

You are a leader of ceremony and divine experiences that bring people together at special times in their lives. You understand the deep importance of acknowledging ourselves as souls having a human experience and all the joy, sadness, growth, challenge and delight that may come with that journey. You are a memory creator for yourself and others in meaningful and beautiful ways.

Life and cycle thresholds such as menarche, pregnancy, birth, death, weddings, graduations, the Wheel of the Year, retirements and so many more are important to you. You desire these life experiences to be acknowledged for the vital role they play in our human experience and the exploration and celebration of our spirituality that come with them. As a priestess you love to celebrate people at special times, especially in a way that helps them make 'sense' of a life experience and move forward with wholeness for all that they have been, all that they are now, and all that they are becoming. In doing so as a ceremonialist, you support them to fully open up to the next phase of their life in a way that has inspired people to pause, reflect and honour themselves, connecting deeply to their spiritual self as they do so.

A natural organiser, you love the process of planning a ceremonial experience and carefully considering every aspect of what that will include. Music, food, games, performance, dance, rituals, traditions and even costumes are all considerations for you in creating and leading a special ceremony for parents naming their newborn baby, a young girl celebrating her menarche, a family honouring the life of a departed loved one, or even the marking of a release and new sense of freedom for someone newly divorced. Each experience inspires in you a desire to learn more about these significant times of our lives and beautiful ways that you can bring forth for them to be acknowledged.

You love showcasing your leadership, warmth, style, gentleness, humour, strength and so much more in times of togetherness, and you hold the role you take in creating powerful space at these important times with deep reverence. This is what you are known for. And are proud to be so.

# The Beautifier Priestess

You make things look, sound, smell and feel beautiful. Which is important, necessary and even life-changing work. Yes, you! The candle lighter, flower arranger and dish-washer. More on those dishes soon!

The environments we create in our work as priestesses have the capacity to inspire, connect and heal. They can support people to feel safe, ignited and ready to change. They are not an afterthought or something we just do to get pretty snaps for Instagram. Their meaning and potential to be a catalyst is much deeper than that. As are the beautifier priestesses who are called to use their talents in this service.

If you are a beautifier priestess, you are someone who willingly cleans and clears spaces with the intent to create an environment that is sacred and in service to all those who experience it. The size of the space is not important. It may be a tiny altar for a gathering of just a few, a sacred circle for a small women's group, a red tent for a community gathering, or a large workshop space or temple that may touch hundreds.

You are the cleaner, candle lighter, flower arranger, oracle deck selector, scent blender, sensory creatrix and mood director. Yours is often the work that people see, smell, touch and feel when they first enter a space that is conducted behind the scenes and often for many hours or even days before arrival. The comfort and joy of others is paramount to you.

Priestesses as beautifiers are also often food gatherers and servers. It's all a part of the sensory experience of being in their presence. They select the herbal teas and raw chocolate with more care than you may imagine and take their role of nourishing you with great reverence. And packing up, clearing up and washing the dishes? All a part of the experience and joy of being in service.

If you know yourself to be a beautifier priestess or wish to explore this side of yourself further, know that what you do in this space truly matters. It is not secondary to those priestesses who may be more 'out front.' Yours is the work that allows them to shine in their role and would often not be possible if it were not for your gifts. Claim the hearth-inspired Goddess Vesta as a part of your sacred gifts knowing that you inspire others as you do so.

# The Veil-Lifter Priestess

You are a veil-lifter and bridge between the worlds of the seen and unseen and spirit and matter. You help people gain clarity, direction and comfort through your intuitive, psychic and clairsentient skills, skills that have been artfully used by priestesses since ancient times.

You may have known you had psychic and intuitive abilities since you were a child and been embracing of them for a long time. Or they may have slowly developed over your lifetime, even bringing up fears about what they mean for you. You are now at a place where you are committed to using your intuitive skills in self-leadership and service by listening to the deepest parts of your soul for guidance. You understand the deep power of stillness, reflection and giving devoted time to yourself and you are potentially clairsentient in many ways. You can attain powerful personal and collective information beyond usual human perception, whether that be through your daily connection to those around you or by attracting them towards you in your career and business. You feel very connected to particular goddesses, gods, angels, animals and other universal energies as they deliver messages and meaning to you in all you do.

If you are clairvoyant, you receive images through your mind's eye via things such as dreams and visions. If you are claircognisant, you 'know' things through your own insight. If clairaudient you hear things without the use of your physical ears and if clairempathic you attune to the emotional experiences of people, animals and places to feel emotions or pain. If you are clairsentient, you obtain insight through your body and physically feeling others' emotions or pain. If you are clairagent, you perceive things about an event or person by contact or proximity to them. If you are clairscent, insights come to you through smell without the use of your physical nose, and if clairgustant you can taste things without putting anything in your mouth.

You are able to use your clairsentient skills in many ways and may be known as a psychic, medium or channel, or simply by any name that calls you. You honour your gifts and those that continue to emerge for you, for the powerful insights, wisdom and healing they bring. You are a beloved messenger of the spirit world and help those having a lived human experience to always know there is something beyond us all.

# The Gatherer and Space-Holder Priestess

You love people and one of your great passions is to gather them together in meaningful and sacred experiences. You are a leader and a catalyst for collective change and transformation. When you gather souls together in spaces you curate, the conditions for personal and group transformation are present.

Your work may take place around a kitchen table, on a picnic rug in a park, at a mother's group, on retreat in a beautiful location, in the wilds of the bush or in a large stadium. You may gather two people, five, twelve, hundreds or thousands. The number does not matter. The container and conditions for change you create does. Your gatherings as a priestess often look like sacred circles, red tents, group meditations, sacred dance parties, music, art or craft workshops, soulful trainings, support groups, transformational retreats and conferences.

You have gifts in the areas of deep listening, communication, both spoken and unspoken, and creating fields of energy that are inclusive and welcoming. And organisation? Definitely organisation! You are a planner, list creator and doer, or you know how to delegate such things for incredible outcomes. You are calm, able to gracefully move between people and situations that may pull your attention in many directions, and fluid in your approach to anything that may happen at a moment's notice.

As a priestess who wants those who come into your spaces to have the most sacred and divine experience possible, you are committed to knowing the very special language and processes that groups go through. You know that people in group settings are not just a collective of individuals. They are both that and the group is an entity of its own which will have ebbs, flows, highs, lows and emotions. You know groups go on very specific journeys where you as the sacred leader must hold powerful space for what is taking place, and what still may be to come.

You will often combine your skills of gathering with other of your priestess skills such as healing, ceremony, beautifying and performing. All come together in your personal magic in ways that have the ability to touch many lives in meaningful ways.

# The Performer and Artist Priestess

You are heart-started by the magic of art, singing, dance and music. And as a priestess performer and artist you know that this magic has the power to transform people's lives, not just in a moment or while your art can be heard or seen, but can be something that lives on with someone forever.

The sharing of your sacred gifts such as song, music, dance and art can act as a spiritual portal for someone to enter into a space of deep meditation, healing and rest. It can also ignite raw passion, physicality and the coming out of someone's wildness within. Divine music or dance can touch someone's heart and drop them into their soul and womb space, helping them feel into their true desires. And the simple act of looking at (let alone creating!) a beautiful piece of art can allow someone to feel into places of magic, mystery and wonder that they often would not be able to if it weren't for the beauty before them.

The power of art, creativity and performance knows no bounds when it comes to the spiritual gifts it can impart. They can ignite in those who do not consider themselves to be creative or musical an incredible sense of belief that they *are* those things in a transformative instant.

After attending my first sacred dance party, I walked away from that electric experience fully claiming I *could* dance. After learning the art of making sacred dolls in one circle gathering, I released decades of false belief that I was not a creative being. After making my own drum and teaching myself slowly and reverently how to work and play with Her, I now proudly say I am a drummer. None of these things mean that as performing as a priestess and artistry are my sacred gifts. They aren't. But what they have shown me is that the priestesses who have guided me to take ownership of these divine acts for myself are living out theirs in the most giving and serving of ways.

Art heals. Music inspires. Song transforms. Dance ignites. All bring joy and hope to our spiritual journeys in a way that so often sees us connect and commune with others in beautiful experiences as well. If you are a priestess performer and artist, or emerging into being one, your work is divine and needed. Long may you play, sing, dance and create.

# The Diviner Priestess

You are a bringer of clarity, hope and insight through the ancient practice of divination, relaying messages and meanings from the spirit realms in service to one's highest self. As a priestess diviner you gain insight into questions and situations through process, ritual and tools that often point you towards something you already knew either about yourself or someone else. This may include seeing what is to come in the future.

Divination has existed in various forms throughout history in many different cultures, religions and spiritual practices, all of which influence you in some form today. There are many different types of divination that you may practice including, but not limited to numerology (divination using numbers), astrology (divination by the positions of the planets, sun and moon), scrying (divination by seeking a vision while gazing into a reflective object such as a crystal ball, fire, mirror or water), pallomancy (divination using a pendulum), cartomancy (divination using a deck of cards), taromancy (divination using a tarot cards), runecasting (divination using runes), and palmistry (divination through reading and interpreting the lines and shape of hands).

Your skills as a diviner are something you harness the power of your intuition and clairsentient gifts for, and that you have developed through repetition, but also likely feel are inherent inside you. You know you have an ability to feel and read into things as a gift from your ancestors, cultural and spiritual lineage. Whether you adore the feel of oracle or tarot cards in your hands, the magic of intense scrying, the infinite wisdom of astrology or the intricacy of reading runes, palms or pendulums, you love to speak to people's lives, hopes, feelings and journeys and where they are right now, where they desire to go and what they are trying to cultivate for themselves.

Your ability to be able to see and interpret greater spiritual and life meaning for those you divine for can bring about much needed affirmation, connection to spirit, creativity, self-care and inner wisdom. Your divination is a catalyst for action that can help people deepen their whole healing and path forward in life in the most meaningful ways.

# The Healer Priestess

You are a space-holder for healing. As a counsellor, coach, reiki master, kinesiologist, masseuse, chakra cleanser, sexuality doula, and potentially so much more, you are here as a priestess to hold space for the healing of humanity. Individually and collectively. Like so many ancient priestesses before you, you feel a calling to be present, witness and help transmute the suffering of others in a way that always centres them as the rightful sovereign of their own being.

You know this is not about you.

And that knowing, in and of itself, could be the core reason why you are not just a counsellor, coach or service provider. That you are both those things and a priestess. You know that your work is not about giving advice or answers, or that somehow, even with all of your expert training, you know what is best for someone. You are fully aware that the space you hold for your healing, even with the gifts you have in multiple areas, is only the container for change that someone who trusts and works with you has stepped into. That the real work and change will always come from the conscious decisions they make to be open, humble, self-giving, radically responsible and centring of their own healing and growth.

As a healer who is walking a path as a priestess you are also deeply aware that your own ongoing healing is of paramount importance in the work you do. You know that you cannot be in deep service if your ego constantly has you worried about what your clients may think of you, if you are doing something 'right', or if they will return for another session. And in thinking and feeling such things you know this does not mean anything is wrong with you, but rather you are experiencing a calling to go within to work on yourself at deeper levels, becoming a more powerful and magic filled healer as a result.

Priestess healers are also fine-tuned to the fact that everything you do with your sacred gifts in service has a spiritual element. The transformational shifts and alchemy that someone undergoes with your care and support is all in service to a soul's spiritual path and evolution. The good. The heartbreaking. The hard. The joyous.

All of it. And then some.

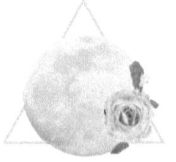

# The Earth-Whisperer Priestess

You are a child of nature. Leaves, trees, flowers, waterfalls, animals, plants, soil and insects—all the gifts of the Great Mother—are a source of delight and even companionship for you. Together with them you know that a part of your life purpose and role is to act as a wayshower for Her in meaningful ways.

You have a natural appreciation and understanding of the healing properties of nature and you desire to both use Her gifts and protect Her in equal measures. You know Her healing powers intimately because they are a constant in your world and a deep part of your own healing path. You are also infinitely curious about nature's wise but sometimes mysterious ways and how they can enhance yours and others lives.

Your earthwhispering and magic come through in the use of things such as crystals, plants, herbs and essential oils. You use these for yourself and others to do things such as create balance in our bodies, help us breathe easier, sleep more soundly, ease pain, calm our central nervous system, aid our meditation practices, support ritual and so much more. You also totally channel goddess energy in the kitchen!

You're a culinary expert when it comes to preparing and cooking vegetables and herbs, and you never met an edible flower that didn't make you swoon!

You also priestess as earth-whisperer through land Herself. You know the deep rejuvenation, invigoration and even joy that can come from swimming in a secluded rock pool, climbing a mountain for a divine view, walking on soft beach sand or lying on a bed of crunchy leaves. You know deep in your own bones that nature is the ultimate healer just as She is, and that simply being with Her enlivens our hearts as we learn to see ourselves reflected in Her beauty and power. Your whispering magic desires you to create a relationship with Her for yourself and others that is reverent, lasting, spiritual and profound.

And we need you now as She needs you more than ever.

Carry on wild child of the forest, rivers, lakes and trees. Carry on.

# PART VII

# Sacred Leadership

All your healing and personal work as a priestess will lead you to your truest and most divine self. Your most divine self that lives life to its fullest and most loving expression. A life where your essence and love can be powerfully seen and felt, and where your soul feels alight with possibilities for how it will help you show up in the world as a sacred spiritual leader.

**Yes.**

**As a priestess you are a sacred spiritual leader.**

A leader who has committed to a personal healing path for life, has a devoted spiritual practice of their own creation and meaning, and openly shares their gifts in service to others and the Great Mother.

This is at the heart of any priestess calling. How can you powerfully harness your own healing and gifts to be in service to the world? And in doing so, support others, especially other women, to find their own connection to their highest and truest self? How can you be a way-shower for others that helps them find their truth and most meaningful spiritual connections?

A leadership path is at the heart of everything you have already done, or will choose to do, if you desire to walk through life as a priestess. It is a core part of the commitment you make to being and living as one, even if you have not realised that up until this very moment. Just like Enheduanna, Fidelm, Mary Magdalene or Fermina Gómez Pastrana maybe did not realise, until they did, either.

What a sacred leadership path may mean or look like for you is yours to uncover. And if you don't see yourself as a leader now or imagine yourself to be one in the future? You are. And the sooner you see that and make a continued commitment to uncovering your own transformational and sacred leadership path the better.

**Because we need you. We need you now more than ever before.**

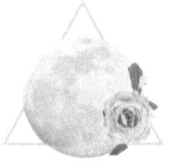

# Are You Talking to Me?

---

Yes, sister. You.

And so, before you get caught up in any preconceived or long-held notions of what 'real' leadership looks like or is all about, take a breath for a moment. Or two … Especially if you're thinking you're not one.

We have been sold a very patriarchal and hierarchical version of leadership for a long time. A version that sees many people believe that being a leader means you must always be out front, bold in voice, extroverted, a charming networker and visibly strong. And undoubtedly that leadership is all about how you influence others and what you can be seen to be doing. These are the primary qualities and behaviours we are often told great leaders hold. And a narrow cycle is often then perpetuated where only people who fit those qualities step into being a leader or are given opportunities to do so.

And when that happens, we all, collectively as humanity, lose. Because leadership is about so much more than these things. So much more. And it's time for many of us, especially as priestesses, to shake off the collective hangover we are holding onto that the primary figure of a great leader is displayed in such ways like a rousing general igniting his troops into action. Great to give you goosebumps at the movies in those pivotal battle scenes. Not so much as an inclusive example of what leadership is and can be.

It's no wonder that many women come to tell themselves stories that feed into the thought they are not now, nor could ever be, a leader. 'I'm not like that.' 'That's not me.' 'I could never do that.' 'I could not inspire in that way.' 'I couldn't lead people like that.' 'I am so not a leader.' And that such stories then conveniently play into keeping many incredible women, including priestesses, held back from knowing their own version of leadership and how it can powerfully and divinely impact others and the wider world.

As a priestess your spiritual leadership begins from within. It's not about anything that can be seen outside of you. It starts and continues and ends with your own healing and the reclaiming and claiming of your wholeness, all that soul work that sees you go within to the deepest parts of you that most need your love and attention. And when you begin to do that personal work you also begin to challenge the patriarchy and other oppressive systems as you do so, stepping out of the binary of what we have come to believe about ourselves as leaders and the narrow definitions and small platforms foisted upon us by societal norms of what true leadership is. We expand our thinking of our own self, abilities, qualities and wholeness as something that has value beyond ourselves and value in a leadership form as well.

At its core, spiritual leadership as a priestess is about your commitment to your own healing and showing up in the world as your full self, honouring your commitments, spiritual practice, and the sharing of your gifts. It is where you embody—every day—the knowledge you have gleaned from your spiritual commitment to self and how you walk through the world with empathy, compassion and sacredness. And where you continue to work on releasing yourself of perfectionism, defensiveness, comparison, or any other part of yourself that shows itself to you on your spiritual journey.

A spiritual leader lives within you. She has a heartbeat and rhythm all of Her own. She has wisdom and power and gentleness and strength and She will show up to you and others in whatever way She is meant to as the living embodiment of your soul's essence and all that you choose to do on this priestess path. She needs no one to tell Her that She must do this or that, or be this way or that way, to be a leader.

She is a sovereign power in Her own right. You are a sovereign power in your own right.

The leader of your own life. In every way. A leader in every way. This I know about any woman who walks a priestess path with commitment, humility and heart.

And so, it's time to drop the story or stories, right? Right. It's time for your sacred leadership to be birthed into the world.

**And so yes, sister. I'm talking to you.**

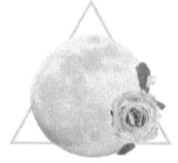

# The Sacred Part

---

Let's take another one of those breaths for a moment.

Okay. I got you. And I know you've got you too!

And so, are we really talking about leadership here or are we really talking about life? A way of life? A way of being?

A large part of me as a priestess in my own life and spiritual journey is believing more readily that spiritual and sacred leadership is a way of being and life that we consciously choose to embody every day. It's not something we decide to lead with on one day, but not another, or that only comes out at certain times, especially when we may be more visible.

Yes. I believe sacred leadership is a way of life for a priestess.

Transformational leadership mentor and research developer Dr Tjanara Goreng Goreng says that leadership is about what we do in everyday life and that it is a consciousness and way of thinking, being and doing that inspires others.[1] Dr Goreng Goreng's work in the area of sacred and Indigenous elder leadership, expanding on the work of Professor Robert Kegan, describes sacred leaders as having a consciousness where they integrate their connection to self, wider relationships, communities and the whole of the planet together, with a deep understanding that the way they show up in the world every day has an impact on all around them.[2]

Dr Goreng Goreng and Professor Kegan's work[3] describes sacred leaders as having many qualities including that they are focused on how everything they do impacts others, that they have high levels of expansive and visionary thinking, that they face challenges and conflicts well, seeking further personal lessons and wisdom as they do, that their unconditional love for themselves, others and the planet is one of their driving forces, and that their spirituality and seeing everything around them as sacred is a core tenant to their leadership and way of life.

This is sacred leadership where core tenants of personal responsibility, love, consciousness, wisdom, love, connection, alignment, and yes, more love again, take centre stage. This is the sacred part. This is sacred leadership that is in fact a sacred life and where deep reverence is paid to the knowing that our impact trumps our intention, (no matter how well intended or not intended at all), every time.

There is nothing about sacred leadership that holds that someone must identify as extroverted or introverted, that means someone has power over others, that they are at 'the top' or in charge all the time, that their's is the only word to be listened to, or that what is trying to be achieved is the most important part of someone's connection to another. This is not leadership that is associated with power, money or superiority, and it is where we are clearly shown that positions of authority are not necessarily positions of leadership. And, in particular, not a position of sacred leadership.

The path of sacred leadership that we walk as a priestess is not a destination to be reached. And in being truthful, maybe many of us will never fully embody what it means to be a sacred leader. I know I am not there and have much work to do. However, I am passionate, excited and committed to try. I know this is not a destination for me to reach, but a journey I am now on in search of sacred meaning in every moment of my life and how I serve others. It is a commitment that I, and you, choose. A commitment where we walk through life in search of our own sacred leader within and how we can bring that forth to best serve all those around us as holders of deep space, spiritual connection and love. As Priestesses.

**It's a path that I walk for life.**

Please, sister, join me. There is room for us all. And I don't wish to journey alone.

# Let's Ride a New (Old) Wave

Do you feel as though leadership in the world right now, especially at the highest levels of visibility, is deeply and sorely lacking? Deeply and sorely lacking in the one thing it should uphold most?

Humanity?

I do.

I could launch into a long tirade of how that is showing itself to us throughout the world in a myriad of ways, but I know I don't need to. You know, and are maybe even directly experiencing it yourself, in everything from the refugee crisis to Indigenous rights to child slavery to desecration of the Great Mother.

A desire for a new paradigm of leadership is stirring deeply in the hearts of so many of us. It's a longing for leadership that is compassionate and holistic and one that values life, empathy, vulnerable truth, and strives to honour the Great Mother through the crisis She, and therefore we, now find ourselves in.

In many ways this 'new' leadership we are looking for could be just a reclaiming of an old one.

It is not a mistake or coincidence that so many of us are longing to return to older ways, connect with our ancestors, slow our pace, disconnect from technology, and dare I say it without sounding like an impending cranky crone, belong to a time where manners, courtesy, care and connection were easier to come by. We only have to talk to our grandparents if we are blessed to still have them, or simply older people around us, to know that such times did exist. And when we think about collective communities of the past where shared leadership and connection was the norm, maybe this should come as no surprise to those of us who have this longing.

**Is everything old, new again?**
**Or do we want everything old to be new again?**

Either way, this deep desire is groaning and growing from the underbelly of the ground we walk on, calling us to uplift ourselves into a higher, deeper and wider way of living and serving each other with humanity at the heart. And when we honour this calling, we will step into full alignment with the type of person we wish to become and the world we want to live in as well. It is where our sacred leadership becomes alight with possibilities and our love and gifts of service will create the new/old paradigm we want to create or return to. Along the way we will see others who want to jump on the waves with us and a tidal wave of new humanity will be birthed.

There are layers upon layers of ways we've gotten ourselves here at this moment in time where we don't see the leadership in politics, education, business, the media and more we want, and therefore there will be many ways we rise up and get ourselves out of it. It will begin however with you as a priestess—along with every other sacred leader throughout the world—working out what *is* the type of leadership you want to see us be inspired by and with it, the type of world you want to live in.

Do you know? Have you taken the time to connect deeply with yourself enough to move beyond just thinking or wishing you want things to be different about your world—our world—and actually work out what you want that difference to look and be like? What do you want to end, shift, move, change? What do you desire to be a part of? What does the world you want to live in look like?

You can't create what you don't have a vision for. And so, it's now time for you to create the space you need to allow that vision to come to life, your vision for yourself and the world. Don't overthink it. Pen. Paper. Dot points. Speak into your phone. Crayon it out. Dance it up. And get ready to take it from vision to action.

Waves crash into the shoreline all the time. And whether or not you catch and ride them is entirely your choice. However, if you want a new paradigm of leadership to ignite the world, then as a priestess you don't really have a choice. You're already riding that wave. How thrilling, igniting, serving, life-changing and extraordinarily meaningful that ride is going to be is now up to you.

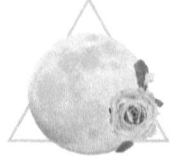

# Beyond Dreaming

If we want a new way of sacred leadership and living to be a part of our everyday and the wider world, it is our responsibility to create it.

And this means that when we see something that is not the way we want it to be or know it can be better and more serving to others and the Great Mother, we as priestesses initiate ourselves into what needs to be done to change it. We don't deflect, turn away or ask someone else to do it. Or just sit back and think that someone will.

**We make it happen.**

You may have experienced the narrow stereotype those who are committed to a spiritual journey can sometimes be portrayed like. Visions of passive, floaty like creatures who lie around in hemp hammocks all day with flower crowns on abound. I'm sure you know what I mean. It's a stereotype that can give the impression that priestesses are cleansing their crystals and oracle card decks on repeat and not actually doing that much that makes a tangible difference. I hope by now you realise that priestesses are action oriented, driven, committed leaders who use their power, rage, compassion and love to bring about positive and meaningful change. And that as one, you are making a commitment to those things too.

And this change can of course come in many forms. It begins with individual healing and addressing our own inherent biases and how they may be contributing to pain or harm in any way, whether we are consciously aware of them or not. This taking of personal responsibility for our own actions is where true change for us all as an entire species and planet begins. You first. Me first. Us first. Before we may charge out waving a placard or protesting or writing letters to politicians. All of which can be amazing catalysts for change but mean very little if we are not doing our own work and looking at where we need to do better and change as well.

And it's when we take responsibility for our own homes and inner worlds that we can move into conscious and embodied action that can make a real difference to us all. That's when our sacred leader emerges and begins to grow with impact.

And I feel deeply in not just my heart, but right down to the marrow of my bones, that it is this kind of action from sacred leaders that is going to be the difference in the world we crave right now. Action orientated, sacred and committed leaders who are constantly doing their own work and healing, while refusing to sit idly by or wishing that someone else would stand up for what they believe and want, but won't embody enough to do anything about. Leaders who have moved out of just dreaming or thinking about things, to actually showing an embodied commitment to the action it takes to make things happen.

The question to your inner sacred leader therefore becomes, what will it take for you to move beyond dreaming about the way you want your world to be for yourself and us all? What will it take for you to do your work? When will you move into action? And how?

You have love, anger, compassion, fire, commitment and drive in your heart as a sacred leader. There are things you want done. Things that you want to be different. Things that you want to be better. Things that you want to leave with greater grace than you found them.

**Dream well, Priestess.**
**But then strap on your boots.**

**There's work to be done.**

# There's No Denying It

We all have privilege in some form.

How can we not as a soul having a lived human experience with all the wondrous things we can be and do in our lives? We absolutely carry privilege in many ways, no matter what story or stories we may have told ourselves otherwise. And acknowledging your privilege and how you can use it to be in service to others is a vital part of your sacred leadership path.

Your privilege as a human being may be present in many forms. Some you may realise and know about, others you may not, but in opening up your sacred leadership path you will have to become aware of them if you're to put that sacred part of this leadership path into full effect.

What we think of as being 'privileged' is something that can be heavily influenced by the patriarchy and capitalism. Many people think that if someone has access to plentiful money, which in turn may mean that they live in a large and comfortable home, have access to excellent education, reliable private transport and more, that they are privileged. And socio-economically, they are.

This in turn can mean that if those desirable aspects of privilege, according to the patriarchy and capitalism, are lacking, then somehow we think someone is not privileged. And it's a part of those oppressive systems that has us believe that wealth is the only form of privilege when it is not. It's very convenient for them to have us keep striving for such things in the way they want us to, because it is the perfect distraction from all other forms of privilege that exist. Such is the blindness that patriarchy, white supremacy and capitalism have, and wish for us to have too.

Privilege comes in many forms other than socio-economic. You have privilege if you are able-bodied and can navigate the world without needing to worry will there be a bathroom you can readily access when in public. You have privilege if you are heterosexual cisgendered and have never had to question your gender identity or be fearful of fully expressing your attraction or love for someone in any way that is not heterosexual. You have privilege if you meet the current societal expectations of beauty standards, especially if you are thin, and do not have to navigate the world in a body that may be fat and the stares, jokes and lack of access to non-discriminatory healthcare that can bring. You are privileged if you are a man and benefit from all the ways the world uplifts you simply because of that, including that you earn more money for the same work done by women, especially Black, Brown, Indigenous and Women of Colour, in many industries.

Most of all you are privileged if you are white.

Regardless of your socio-economic status, body type, ableness, gender or sexual identity, if you are white you carry the most powerful privilege that exists. You were born into the social norm of what the world currently upholds at its centre. You can open a magazine or turn on the television and will see a majority of people who look like you. You will not have had the history of your people or culture erased throughout your education. You will rarely, if ever, be the only white person in a room. You will not be discriminated against on sight based on your skin colour or race in everything from access to healthcare, job interviews or being served in a restaurant. You do not have to worry you will be racially profiled or targeted by the police.

Does this mean your life is without incident, heartache, challenges and difficulties? No. Not in any way. However, so often I have been witness to people when confronted with their white privilege fling back with 'I have it hard too', like they're in some kind of competition for who can claim to be the most oppressed. Well, no matter how hard you think you have had it, if you walk through the world as a white person you carry more privilege and power than anyone else who does not, regardless of any other circumstances in your life. I did not grow up with socio-economic privilege—we were poor and on welfare—and I have lived most of my life in a fat body. I missed out on school camps, worked four minimum wage jobs to get by as a teen and endured teasing, bullying and discrimination based on my body type. But I'm white. And, therefore, cannot hang my hat on any ridiculous notion that I have had a life that is as complex and filled with racism, discrimination, and ongoing verbal and behavioural hostilities (known as micro-aggressions, despite their impact not being micro in any way), in comparison to someone who has not.

Denial of white privilege is futile, bypassing and racist. Ownership of it means you open up the capacity for yourself to do something with that privilege that is powerful and life changing for yourself and others in ways you may never have realised you could.

# Power and Privilege

So you have privilege. Got it. What now are you going to do with it?

This is not for me to say. I'm not a social justice educator or expert, and of course, I don't know the intricacies of your life. This is for you to find out and decide as a part of your life path and commitment to being a priestess. This doesn't mean, however, that you need to research and put things into action on your own. In fact, that's not recommended at all.

If anything I've mentioned about privilege, white supremacy, race, ableism and more has you reeling or even just questioning where you begin, then the best place is going to be through educating yourself. It's tempting to want to race out and start 'doing' all the things you think are necessary, but that's likely the worst thing you can do to begin with and where you may cause harm, which none of us want to do.

If you're only just waking up to your privilege and the many ways in which others don't have it as you do, it's time to hit the books, start following social media accounts that speak to areas you need to know more in, and pay for the work of coaches, consultants and educators who can support you to get a grasp on your privileged intersections and how you can powerfully use them as a sacred leader. When you do, know that you cannot receive this education from anyone other than those who are having the lived experience you are not. You cannot learn and do better with matters of racial justice from anyone other than a person who is Black, Brown, Indigenous or a Person of Colour. You cannot be educated about matters of ableism and disability by someone who is not fully able-bodied and can speak directly to that. You cannot hope to learn what it is like to walk through the world having your sexuality or gender questioned every day from someone who does not identify as lesbian, gay, bisexual, transgender, queer or intersex.

And your following, uplifting the voices of and paying these educators is a huge part of the actual redressing of balance and money that for far too long has only flowed to those who carry the most privilege. And so don't underestimate how this educative work is not only truly foundational, but truly life-giving as well.

Know that as you do this work you will likely come up against pushbacks that will seem innocent on the surface but are laced with danger. One of the most popular is people stating they don't 'see colour' and that we are all the same. And the irony here is that these people who often consider themselves to not be racist in the least, by believing in this, show themselves to be exactly that. If someone cannot see how the lived experience of Black, Brown, Indigenous and People of Colour is different from that of white people because of their skin colour and racial appearance, they are in complete denial of the microaggressions, racism and discrimination non-white people face every day. It's spiritual bypassing. And it's racist. When you refuse to see the reality of a person right in front of you and listen to their voices and stories of how oppressive systems and behaviours harm them daily, you deny the truth.

Educating yourself is just the start of your journey as a sacred leader in this realm. It can't be the end. If you truly want to be anti-racist, anti-ableist, anti-homophobic and so much more, you have to call people out, including family and friends, when they drop racist jokes at the dinner table, push back at anyone that thinks it's unfair more disabled car parking spots are being made at your local car park, mock drag queens, make sweeping statements that all crimes are committed by Black youths, cry foul that refugees are taking away jobs from hard-working folk who were there before them, support businesses that are openly homophobic or anti-trans and more. And if you do these things yourself then you begin with you.

This is where you start but not end. You don't take over the work of anyone else with a marginalised identity or start thinking you can teach others how to address such things. You do your own work of looking at your privilege and how it can be used to redress power imbalances, constantly knowing that there is always more to learn and ways to do better. If everyone did this and kept committing to doing more, everything would change. Everything. In service to the world we are all craving.

It's not too big and you saying you don't know what to do is a lie. You do. As a priestess you are a compassionate and giving soul with so much to offer. You have a role to play here in ending suffering, challenging oppressive systems, and ripping down power imbalances that harm us all.

Big work? Yes. But don't say you don't know what to do.
You do. And you can do it.
Start or continue today. I'm right there with you.

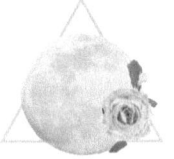

# True Love and Connection

**We are all one.**

I'm sure you have heard this many times, and everyone from scientist Albert Einstein, Jesuit priest Pierre Teilhard de Chardin, visionary Suzy Kassem and poet Kamand Kojouri have all proclaimed in their work it to be so. And it is true genetically, through our DNA, that we are all connected to each other and that our bodies are so similar in the way they bleed, breathe and love.

Spiritual oneness takes our sense of connectedness much further, however, to a place where we come to embrace all states of our awareness, experiences and feelings. To know that we are all connected as human beings to each other and to the pulse of every living creature, plant, rock, tree and raindrop throughout the universe. To know that our choices are much smaller, but also much bigger than our minds could ever comprehend, and possibly only our hearts and souls can truly know. And so yes. We are all one. And we may believe or even deeply know that, but do our actions then support that belief and knowing?

For many they do not.

If our proclamation of oneness only extends to those who are like us, or we understand or feel comfortable with, we've got barriers up that in fact say the opposite. They say you are different from me or I don't understand or trust you. Or even I am afraid of you and you are a threat to me. Even though no such fear is warranted or threat existing. If we are truly going to believe in our oneness as human beings, we must commit to knowing and embodying that especially for those who look, live and are different from ourselves.

And so even though we claim we are one, we in fact ignore people when they say they are hurting from systemic oppressions we may, even inadvertently, be upholding. We also turn a blind eye to animal cruelty. We buy fast fashion even though we know it enslaves people in unsafe working conditions, paid well below a living wage. We push back when we are told something is racist, ableist or transphobic, denying the lived reality of people having a direct experience of it. We know we can make small and big changes to offer greater support and care to the Great Mother and yet we continue to do what we have always done.

And so none of us can say we truly believe 'we are all one', all connected, all in this together, until we are prepared for our actions to line up with that statement. For our sacred integrity as priestesses to be at the forefront with what this truly means. Which is not about being perfect, exemplary, or not having boundaries that protect us from harm. It's about opening up our minds, hearts and souls beyond the glossy façade of 'spiritual speak' that would have us believe because someone says we are all one, that they are then acting in a way that shows an absolutely loving and comprehensive understanding of what that means.

If you look around at your life, career and business and quickly realise that everyone you are surrounded by looks like you and is of the same cultural background and class, you're not truly there when it comes to embodying us all being one. That's just we are all one if you look like me and I am comfortable with you. You have to expand your connection and ability to love and be there for others in genuine and very real ways every day. For me this looks like believing my family members and friends who hold a marginalised identity when they tell me about their lived experiences, and educating myself on ways I can dismantle the systems that harm them. It involves me showcasing diverse voices on my podcast and wider work and being their patrons and clients. It sees me go to events that challenge me to look at my consumption, behaviour and ethics when it comes to all I do and how my decisions impact others and the world around me. It's not all it could be. It's just a start.

Our white-dominated, patriarchal and capitalist world wants to keep us separate, individual and distanced from each other. It doesn't want us to understand each other or be deeply connected, because in doing so we will radically change the world through our compassion and greater understanding of each others' lived experiences. We will truly come to know what it means to be one and the lengths we will then go to see another's pain as our own and do all we can to reduce the harm we bring to all other living souls.

It is once again as priestesses where another ignition point of our sacred leadership and calling comes into the spotlight.

# Protecting Her, Honouring Them

The more we are distanced and disconnected from nature the more we are distanced from an incredible part of ourselves and each other. And if ever there was a leadership commitment we could all make together as humanity to bring us closer it will be one that strives to address this.

In the times of the ancients, being disconnected from nature was not possible. The Great Mother was all and connection, worship of and working with Her dictated someone's very survival. And while we know that nature is inherent in all of us, it's not a stretch to say that many people in our modern world do not realise this or even scoff at such a thing in a failure to understand how deeply connected we are to every part of the land we walk on and how She provides for us every day. Indeed, that we are dependent upon for survival.

What has changed about our relationship with the Great Mother and our view of survival in relation to Her today? Have we reached a point where we believe we no longer need or rely upon Her for our very lives? If one closely examines our behaviour of destruction and the deep oppressiveness of white supremacy, patriarchy, capitalism, environmental destruction and more, then one would think we do no longer believe this. If we look closely, feel deeply, and access both our rational mind and wisest intuition however we know that things are not that different at all. Our survival still depends on Her. In every way.

There are those who say that so many of our modern ills are due to disconnection from Her. Lack of communion and belief in Her. Lack of right relation with Her. Lack of being with Her. Lack of seeing ourselves as a part of Her. This is a deep truth that many of us are beginning to feel or already acutely are. And I believe that is the collective power of women and their sacred leadership who will return us back to Her. Along with our children who are and will continue to beg us to do better by them and the future Earth they will inhabit.

The call to protect, honour, support and care for Her as a spiritual life force is not new. Indigenous people around the world have been begging us to listen and heed their warnings to do exactly that for eons. Any modern-day environmental activism is built on their backs, bleeding hearts and the very lives of their people displaced, separated and murdered for the destructive force that is colonisation. They have been telling us and showing us in their gentle, reciprocal and powerful way of living that all land is sacred and that we should take more reverent care of Her as our home.

There is no belief in the protection and preservation of the earth—Her rights—without protection and preservation of Indigenous rights as well. If your call to humanity and survival only extends to Her, it does not extend enough. The heart of sacred leadership in this area of our lives as priestesses is to know and see the entire picture of the impact we have not just on the land we live with, but if not Indigenous to land ourselves, to those who have been displaced from where we are.

Recycle. Compost. Buy ethically. Reduce your impact in every way you can and build a loving, honest and giving relationship with Her.

Take it up, right up, to the businesses, organisations, corporates, politicians and oppressive systems that pillage Her every day in the name of profit and gain. Demand, shout, rage for them to do better by Her and us all. Now. And every day after.

And commit to raising the voices, listening to the pleas and paying the people who have come before us and have been trying to be our teachers as the traditional custodians of the land we now live on for centuries. Honour, listen and support them in all they say, do and need when it comes to the earth that is such a vital part of their spiritual lives, culture and very way of life.

**Our sacred leadership and everything we do for Her is incomplete without doing so.**

# Are You All In?

So, there's something that often happens when you rise up. Something that is almost inevitable when you step into a bigger purpose for yourself as a sacred leader, especially if you're committed to questioning the status quo and using your privilege, which as a sacred leader you must. It doesn't happen all the time. And it may not happen to you. But it might. Okay, it probably will.

**Deep breath.**

You're going to ruffle some feathers. Things you say or do may rub the 'wrong' way. You might get people riled up. You could even be heavily criticised online or trolled. People that were once connected to you may drop off, silently or with spectacular noise. And if you're white and needing to work through what holding that privilege and your inherent race biases means, you will likely at some point in time be called in or out for something that you're not doing well. As I have. And as may happen with any other privilege you hold.

And it's all okay. You will live. And come through it hopefully a stronger, more informed, compassionate and sovereign priestess who is showing herself to be someone who is continually open to learning and moving beyond any grip of perfectionism, fear of making mistakes, or losing people for the sake of keeping the peace or holding false power. It's okay to feel overwhelmed, out of your depth or uncomfortable on this path, and many times I've been there and will be again. You don't and never will walk alone. But you can't stop.

We have to take stock and look deep within if we are so fragile and we stop doing something as important as this leadership work just because someone disagrees with, points out an error we've made, or challenges us to do better. This is classic patriarchal perfection and white supremacy in action. They want us to fail and feel so small that we think we cannot make a difference. They want us to question our inherent value and worth with the eventual outcome being we remain silent, keep the status quo and continue to do their bidding so that the world order where white men hold the balance of power in all aspects of our lives remains intact.

If we're going to win and create a world that is just and free for us all, those with the most privilege have got to do the heavy lifting and if criticised, called out, or even simply questioned, not drop what their lifting and say, 'This is too hard. I'm out.' Those who do not carry the same privileges are not afforded the same option.

You can't *not* show up in the world every day in the skin you're in, or the wheelchair that carries you, or in the body you inhabit. Therefore, any uncomfortable experience you may have as a sacred leader trying to redress imbalances in the world is nothing in comparison to what others with these lived experiences and many more go through every day. Nothing. And therefore, it is inexcusable of anyone who is a priestess and sacred leader to opt out here in any way.

If you're really all in, nothing that happens to you by way of criticism or rejection will deter you from your sacred leadership duties and path. Sure, it may sting, and you will need to look, with as much self-love and compassion as possible, at yourself and where you can do better and learn more, but this is what it means to commit and go the whole way. And be in deep integrity.

And believe me when I tell you that for anyone you lose along the way of this path if you remain fully committed and on it, you will gain more. Leave them to their business, criticism, defensiveness and anything else that your work here may arise in them. Just do you. Follow what you know to be right. Understand that you can influence the opinion of no one else but yourself. Become committed to uncomfortableness, not knowing what is ahead, forging something new and using your privilege for good.

Are you truly in and ready to go the whole way? Are you ready to walk through life as a priestess and sacred leader *for* life?

Then let's do this. Together we can. And as you do remember this one thing.

**It's not about you when people throw poo.**

It's about them. And you've got too much work to do to get caught up in it. Your focus needs to be on you and the sacred work you're here to do.

# You Are Your Purpose

How are you, sister? I'm truly asking. And I hope you will lovingly ask it of yourself too.

You might be feeling a range of emotions right now including a touch overwhelmed, fired up, lost and unsure, or indeed incredibly found and sure, ready to ignite your life and leadership in a way it never has been before.

All are valid and worthy of your attention and a part of your unfolding path as a priestess. Everything you are feeling and thinking for yourself is you honing and coming to trust your inner guidance at even deeper levels about what your spiritual self truly means to you.

This is where many questions pertaining to your sacred leadership may begin to arise for you, such as:

>Who am I?
>Why am I here?
>What am I meant to do?
>Who is the real me?
>How am I meant to serve?

They are beautiful questions. Rich, deep questions that you taking the time to explore and seek the answers to could be, and likely will be, a lifelong journey. I know they are for me.

If you begin to ask yourself questions like this, please don't expect answers to come to you in a blinding flash or be finite. They may or may be, but our lives are constantly unfolding, and so are the answers or insights that are right for us at any given time. We are constantly changing, alchemising and healing, and so what is true for us in one moment, let alone one year, may not be in another.

I often see, read and hear people say they are looking for their life purpose, many of which these questions allude to. Or that even others encourage them to do so. Take this quiz to find your life purpose! Enrol in this webinar and your life purpose will come to you!

They are seeking, sometimes very strongly, the reason for why they exist, trying to find meaning for their life and what it is they are meant to do. At times, it seems as though they are on a specific hunt or expedition, but I'm not sure that is how you find your life purpose.

Or, indeed, if it is even something to be found, but rather it is something to be lived.

I believe your life is about your full soul expression. Living in alignment with your values, passions and loves. Healing yourself. Making precious moments meaningful. Accepting what is. Changing what can be better. Being joyful.

**Just being.**

And it's in this living—simply living—that your purpose will reveal itself to you. Not in a thunderclap or lightning bolt, but more likely in a gentle opening and trickle from your heart to where you feel most alive, and true to yourself and spiritual path as a priestess every day. To a place where you come to realise that your purpose in life is to be your whole and most true self. To simply be yourself.

When you show up in the world as your whole self you are living your purpose. Every day. In every way. You are doing what you came here to do and that is to show yourself as a divine reflection of the Universe only you, and no one else, can be.

**There is no need for you to look for your purpose.
You are your purpose.**

And all of us, your family, friends, sisters, communities, animal and plant friends, the Great Mother and Universe see you and honour you exactly as you are. We take your purpose to be exactly what we need too and as you step into your own wholeness and self you inspire us to do the same.

# Your Life Is Your Legacy

Imagine for a moment living as your whole self and inspiring someone, or even many someones, to do the same. That's a legacy.

We can often get caught up in the belief that to be the sort of person that leaves a legacy we need to have achieved grand and monumental things such as opening a school, inventing a medicinal cure or starting a movement for radical change. We can even attribute a legacy to only being about things such as bold acts of bravery like putting out a fire or saving someone's life. All of these things are of course important, and we want people to keep doing them, but they're not the only things that make up a legacy-filled life.

We don't have to be famous, be on the news, or have people know us for something to leave a legacy. Your life is your legacy. Everything you do, contribute to, are a part of and make better, is a part of the legacy of your life. The choices that you make every day are a part of the mark you leave on the world. Their size or impact is not what needs to be scrutinised or compared and no major feats are required.

When I think about legacy, I often think of my mum, who is now in her seventies. To many, from the outside looking in, and in the ways we so often measure success in life, she could be seen to have lived a rather uneventful and ordinary life.

She was the second of four born into a struggling farming family, leaving school at fourteen years of age due to chronic illness. She held one paying job before getting married, having two children, getting divorced, and becoming a single mother on welfare with no child support to assist. After moving back to the family farm, she lived with her parents and children, helping to work their land and being involved in her local community until she remarried in later life. Until recently when he passed, she visited her bed-ridden husband in an aged care facility every day where she lives in a country town, where she is also a grandmother and full-time carer to two granddaughters, three cats and a dog.

Mum has never been given an award or had a newspaper article written about her. She's never built anything that can be seen by others or can have a plaque put on it. She's not famous or known for anything.

However, through my clearly biased and loving eyes, I see a woman who is living out a legacy that is far-reaching in so many ways. That one job she held was caring for babies and toddlers, many of whom were disabled and had special needs. That community she was a part of saw her volunteer thousands of hours of her time to programs and initiatives that supported girls, teenagers and the environment. Her recipes for golden syrup dumplings, peppermint slice and sponge cake have made countless home cooks wonder if they may be related to Nigella. Her descendants are carrying out work that touches the lives of tens of thousands of women, especially in ways that see them make money in extraordinary meaningful ways and create their own version of freedom and a sovereign life.

And above all else, through a life that at many points may have completely broken others, she has held kindness, humility, joy, service and love in her heart that has been, and always will be, the most profoundly beautiful and impactful influence in my life. That's a legacy.

Just as your life is your legacy in everything you do. You don't need to do anything in particular to leave an indelible heart print on the world. You just need to be you and live out your purpose as you. If we all chose to do this for ourselves and supported each other to do it as well, we will fulfil our spiritual destiny as souls having a fully human experience on Earth. We will become the priestesses that our world longs for right now.

To live a life as a priestess is to know that your life, legacy and purpose —which you now know to all be the same thing—are, at any moment, worthy of your utmost love, attention and commitment. That you are worthy of your love, attention and commitment.

Everything you need to fulfil your purpose and live your legacy is with you.

Go well, sister.

I see you.

I honour you.

I love you for all that you are right now and all that your divine purpose will bring to the world in your days to come.

## Part I
### Her Living, Her Retreating, Her Rising

¹ Anthony, D. W. (2007) *The horse, the wheel, and language: How Bronze-Age riders from the Eurasian steppes shaped the modern world.* Princeton, NJ: Princeton University Press.

² Lerner, G. (1986) *The creation of patriarchy.* New York: Oxford University Press.

## Part II
### Priestesses Past to Present

¹ Mark, J. J. (2014) 'Daily life in ancient Mesopotamia' *Ancient History Encyclopedia.* Available from: https://www.ancient.eu/article/680/

² Ibid.

³ Podany, A. H. and McGee, M. (2005) *The ancient Near Eastern world.* Oxford: Oxford University Press.

⁴ Bertman, S. (2005) *Handbook to life in ancient Mesopotamia.* Oxford; New York: Oxford University Press.

⁵ Ibid.

⁶ Perot, F. (2008) *The re-emergence of the divine feminine and its significance for spiritual, psychological and evolutionary growth.* Universal Publishers, p. 18.

⁷ Nicholson, S. J. (1989) *The Goddess re-awakening: The feminine principle today.* 1st ed. Wheaton, IL: Theosophical Publishing House, p. 30.

⁸ Klenke, K. (1996) *Women and leadership: A contextual perspective.* New York: Springer, p. 30.

⁹ Perot, F. (2008) *The re-emergence of the divine feminine and its significance for spiritual, psychological and evolutionary growth.* Universal Publishers.

¹⁰ Mark, J. J. (2017) 'Clergy, priests & priestesses in ancient Egypt' *Ancient*

*History Encyclopedia.* Available from: https://www.ancient.eu/article/1026/

[11] Ibid.

[12] Mark, J. J. (2012) 'The Eleusinian Mysteries: The rites of Demeter' *Ancient History Encyclopedia.* Available from: https://www.ancient.eu/article/32/

[13] Ibid.

[14] Cartwright, M. (2019) 'Artemis' *Ancient History Encyclopedia.* Available from: https://www.ancient.eu/artemis/

[15] Mark, J. J. (2009) 'Ephesus' *Ancient History Encyclopedia.* Available from: https://www.ancient.eu/ephesos/

[16] Cartwright, M. (2019) 'Artemis' *Ancient History Encyclopedia.* Available from: https://www.ancient.eu/artemis/

[17] Ibid.

[18] Hughes, J. D. (1990) 'Artemis: Goddess of conservation', *Forest & Conservation History*, vol. 34, no. 4, pp. 191-197.

[19] Gimbutas, M. and Dexter, M. R. (2001) *The living goddesses.* Berkeley, CA: University of California Press, p. 157.

[20] Scott, M. (2014) *Delphi: A history of the center of the ancient world.* Princeton, NJ: Princeton University Press.

[21] Aldhouse-Green, M. J. (1995) *Celtic goddesses: Warriors, virgins and mothers.* London: British Museum Press.

[22] MacLeod, S. P. (2013) *The divine feminine in ancient Europe: Goddesses, sacred women, and the origins of western culture.* Jefferson, NC: McFarland.

[23] MacLeod, S. P. (2012) *Celtic myth and religion: A study of traditional belief, with newly translated prayers, poems, and songs.* London: McFarland, p. 28.

[24] National Museum of Denmark (2019) *The seeresses of the Viking period.* Available from: https://en.natmus.dk/historical-knowledge/denmark/prehistoric-period-until-1050-ad/the-viking-age/religion-magic-death-and-rituals/viking-seeresses/ [Accessed 24 October 2019].

[25] Mitchell, S. A. (2011) *Witchcraft and magic in the Nordic Middle Ages.* Philadelphia, PA: University of Pennsylvania Press.

[26] Blain, J. (2002) *Nine worlds of seid-magic: Ecstasy and neo-shamanism in North European paganism.* London and New York: Routledge.

[27] Rysdyk, E. C. (2016) *The Norse Shaman: Ancient spiritual practices of the northern tradition*. Rochester, VT: Destiny Books.

[28] National Museum of Denmark (2019) *The seeresses of the Viking period*. Available from: https://en.natmus.dk/historical-knowledge/denmark/prehistoric-period-until-1050-ad/the-viking-age/religion-magic-death-and-rituals/viking-seeresses/ [Accessed 24 October 2019].

[29] Norse Mythology for Smart People (2019) 'Freya' *Norse mythology for smart people*. Available from: https://norse-mythology.org/gods-and-creatures/the-vanir-gods-and-Goddesses/freya/ [Accessed 24 October 2019].

[30] History.com Editors (2009) 'Maya' *History*. Available from: https://www.history.com/topics/ancient-americas/maya [Accessed 3 December 2019].

[31] Rogoff, B. (2011) *Developing destinies: A Mayan midwife and town*. New York: Oxford University Press, pp. 164–166.

[32] Encyclopedia.com (2019) 'Gender and religion: Gender and Mesoamerican religions' *Encyclopedia.com*. Available from: https://www.encyclopedia.com/environment/encyclopedias-almanacs-transcripts-and-maps/gender-and-religion-gender-and-mesoamerican-religions [Accessed 24 October 2019].

[33] Nelson, S. M. (2003) *Ancient queens: Archaeological explorations*. Walnut Creek, CA: Altamira Press.

[34] Mineo, L. (2016) 'Where women once ruled' *Harvard Gazette*. Available from: https://news.harvard.edu/gazette/story/2016/07/where-women-once-ruled. [Accessed 23 October 2019].

[35] Encyclopedia.com (2019) 'Gender and religion: Gender and Mesoamerican religions' *Encyclopedia.com*. Available from: https://www.encyclopedia.com/environment/encyclopedias-almanacs-transcripts-and-maps/gender-and-religion-gender-and-mesoamerican-religions [Accessed 24 October 2019].

[36] Ross, J. C. and Steadman, S. R. (2017) *Ancient complex societies*. New York: Routledge, Taylor & Francis Group.

[37] Benson, E. P. and Cook, A. G. (2001) *Ritual sacrifice in ancient Peru*. Austin: University of Texas Press.

[38] Ashcraft-Eason, L., Martin, D. C. and Olademo, O. (2009) *Women and new and Africana religions*. Santa Barbara, CA: Praeger.

[39] Anderson, J. E. (2015) *The Voodoo encyclopedia: Magic, ritual, and religion*. Santa Barbara, CA: ABC-CLIO, LLC.

[40] Shaw, S. M. (2018) *Women's lives around the world: A global encyclopedia.* Santa Barbara, CA: ABC-CLIO, LLC.

[41] Keller, R. S., Ruether, R. R. and Cantlon, M. (2006) *The encyclopedia of women and religion in North America.* Bloomington, IN: Indiana University Press.

[42] Shaw, S. M. (2018) *Women's lives around the world: A global encyclopedia.* Santa Barbara, CA: ABC-CLIO, LLC.

[43] Mason, M. A. (2002) *Living Santería: Rituals and experiences in an Afro-Cuban religion.* Washington, DC: Smithsonian Institution Press.

[44] Fanthorpe, R. L. and Fanthorpe, P. A. (2008) *Mysteries and secrets of Voodoo, Santeria and Obeah.* Toronto: Dundurn Press.

[45] Miller, T. (1995) *America's alternative religions.* Albany, NY: State University of New York Press.

## Part III
### *Power Priestesses*

[1] Roberts, J. (2004) 'Enheduanna, daughter of King Sargon: Princess, poet, priestess (2300 B.C.)' *Transoxiana.org.* Available from: http://www.transoxiana.org/0108/roberts-enheduanna.html.

[2] Grande, L. (2017) *Curators: Behind the scenes of natural history museums.* Chicago, IL: University of Chicago Press.

[3] Ellis, P. B. (1995) *Celtic women: Women in Celtic society and literature.* London: Constable.

[4] MacLeod, S. P. (2012) *Celtic myth and religion: A study of traditional belief, with newly translated prayers, poems, and songs.* London: McFarland, p. 185.

[5] Gera, D. L. (1997) *Warrior women: The anonymous* Tractatus de mulieribus. New York and Leiden: E. J. Brill.

[6] Bogucki, P. (2008) *Encyclopedia of society and culture in the ancient world.* New York: Facts on File, Inc.

[7] MacLeod, S. P. (2013) *The divine feminine in ancient Europe: Goddesses, sacred women, and the origins of western culture.* Jefferson, NC: McFarland.

[8] Connelly, J. B. (2007) *Portrait of a priestess: Women and ritual in ancient Greece*. Princeton, NJ: Princeton University Press.

[9] Chrystal, P. (2017) *Women in ancient Greece: Seclusion, exclusion, or illusion?* Stroud: Fonthill Media.

[10] Smith, B. G. (194-2008) *The Oxford encyclopedia of women in world history*. Oxford: Oxford University Press.

[11] Adams Media (2017) *The book of Celtic myths: From the mystic might of the Celtic warriors to the magic of the fey folk, the storied history and folklore of Ireland, Scotland, Brittany, and Wales*. Avon, MA: Adams Media.

[12] Mark, J. J. (2013) 'Boudicca' *Ancient History Encyclopedia*. Available from: https://www.ancient.eu/Boudicca/

[13] Salisbury, J. E. (2001) *Encyclopedia of women in the ancient world*. Santa Barbara, CA: ABC-CLIO.

[14] Adams Media (2017) *The book of Celtic myths: From the mystic might of the Celtic warriors to the magic of the fey folk, the storied history and folklore of Ireland, Scotland, Brittany, and Wales*. Avon, MA: Adams Media, p. 90.

[15] Koch, J. T. (2006) *Celtic culture: A historical encyclopedia*. Santa Barbara, CA: ABC-CLIO.

[16] Monaghan, P. (2004) *The encyclopedia of Celtic mythology and folklore*. New York: Facts on File, Inc.

[17] Editors of Encyclopedia Britannica (2018) 'Saint Mary Magdalene' *Encyclopædia Britannica*. Available from: https://www.britannica.com/biography/Saint-Mary-Magdalene

[18] Encyclopedia.com (2019) 'Mary Magdalene' *Encyclopedia.com*. Available from: https://www.encyclopedia.com/people/philosophy-and-religion/biblical-proper-names-biographies/mary-magdalene

[19] Barclay, W. (1968) *The New Testament: A new translation*. London and New York: Collins.

[20] Fraschetti, A. (2001) *Roman women*. English language ed. Chicago: University of Chicago Press.

[21] Kraemer, R. S. (2004) *Women's religions in the Greco-Roman world: A sourcebook*. New York: Oxford University Press.

22. Editors of Encyclopaedia Britannica (2019) 'Saint Brigid of Ireland' *Encyclopædia Britannica*. Available from: https://www.britannica.com/biography/Saint-Brigit-of-Ireland [Accessed 30 October 2019].

23. Wright, B. (2009) *Brigid: Goddess, druidess and saint*. Stroud: The History Press.

24. Depuis, N. (2009) *Mná na hÉireann: Women who shaped Ireland*. Cork: Mercier Press.

25. Editors of Encyclopaedia Britannica (2019a) 'Brigit, Celtic deity' *Encyclopædia Britannica*. Available from: https://www.britannica.com/topic/Brigit

26. Healy, J. (2013) 'Catholic Encyclopedia (1913)/School of Kildare' *Wikisource*. Available from: https://en.wikisource.org/wiki/Catholic_Encyclopedia_(1913)/School_of_Kildare

27. Appiah, A. and Gates, H. L. (2005) *Africana: The encyclopedia of the African and African American experience*. 2nd ed. Oxford; New York: Oxford University Press.

28. Salmonson, J. A. (1992) *The encyclopedia of Amazons: Women warriors from antiquity to the modern era*. New York: Anchor Books.

29. Lynch, P. A. and Roberts, J. (2010) *African mythology, A to Z*. 2nd ed. New York: Chelsea House Publishers.

30. Ilahiane, H. (2017) *Historical dictionary of the Berbers (Imazighen)*. 2nd ed. Lanham, MD: Rowman & Littlefield.

31. Becker, C. (2015) 'Dihya: The female face of Amazigh history' *Amazigh World News*. Available from: https://amazighworldnews.com/dihya-the-female-face-of-amazigh-history/

32. Ward, M. (2004) *Voodoo queen: The spirited lives of Marie Laveau*. Jackson, MS: University Press of Mississippi.

33. Long, C. M. (2006) *A New Orleans voudou priestess: The legend and reality of Marie Laveau*. Gainsville, FL: University Press of Florida.

34. Fandrich, I. J. (2016) *The mysterious voodoo queen, Marie Laveaux: A study of powerful female leadership in nineteenth century New Orleans*. London: Routledge.

35. Mazama, A. (2019) 'Charwe: Shona spiritual leader' *Encyclopædia Britannica*. Available from: https://www.britannica.com/biography/Charwe

[Accessed 30 October 2019].

[36] Akyeampong, E. K. and Gates, H. L., Jr. (2011) *Dictionary of African biography.* Oxford and New York: Oxford University Press.

[37] Asante, M. K. and Mazama, A. (2009) *Encyclopedia of African religion.* Los Angeles, CA: Sage.

[38] Rain Queens of Africa (2011) 'Mbuya Nehanda a.k.a. Charwe Nyakasikana: My bones shall rise again' *Rain Queens of Africa.* Available from: http://rainqueensofafrica.com/2011/03/mbuya-nehanda-a-k-a-charwe-nyakasikana-%E2%80%9Cmy-bones-shall-rise-again%E2%80%9D/ [Accessed 30 October 2019].

[39] Google.com (2019) *Google Translate.* Available from: https://translate.google.com/translate?hl=en&sl=es&u=https://www.ecured.cu/Fermina_G%25C3%25B3mez&prev=search

[40] Brown, D. H. (2003) *Santería enthroned: Art, ritual, and innovation in an Afro-Cuban religion.* Chicago, IL: University of Chicago Press.

[41] Canizares, R. (1993) *2002 Santería Cubana: El Sendero de la Noche.* Mexico: Lasser Press Mexicana.

[42] Beliso-de J. A. (2019) 'View of Santería copresence and the making of African diaspora bodies' *Cultural Anthropology.* Available from: https://journal.culanth.org/index.php/ca/article/view/ca29.3.04/315 [Accessed 30 October 2019].

[43] Pérez, E. (2016) Religion in the kitchen: Cooking, talking, and the making of Black Atlantic traditions. New York: New York University Press.

## Part V
### *Living Embodied*

[1] Mark, J. J. (2019) 'Wheel of the Year' *Ancient History Encyclopedia.* Available from: https://www.ancient.eu/Wheel_of_the_Year/

[2] Editors of Encyclopedia Britannica (2013) 'Lunar calendar' *Encyclopædia Britannica.* Available from: https://www.britannica.com/science/lunar-calendar

[3] Willison, C. (2018) *An introduction to storytelling.* Stroud: The History Press.

[4] Online Etymology Dictionary (2019) 'Moon' *Online Etymology Dictionary.* Available from: https://www.etymonline.com/word/moon [Accessed 30 October 2019].

[5] The Latin Dictionary (2010) 'Mensis' *The Latin Dictionary.* Available from: http://latindictionary.wikidot.com/noun:mensis

[6] Davis, E. (2010) 'Blood mysteries' *Elizabethdavis.com.* Available from: https://elizabethdavis.com/blood-mysteries/. Excerpt from: Davis, E. and Leonard, C. (1996) *The women's wheel of life: Thirteen archetypes of woman at her fullest power.* New York: Viking Arkana.

[7] The Kalasha Bashali (n.d.) Available from: https://www.press.umich.edu/pdf/0472097830-05.pdf. Excerpt from Maggi, W. R. (2001) *Our women are free: Gender and ethnicity in the Hindukush.* Ann Arbor, MI: University of Michigan Press.

[8] Sturm, C. (2002) *Blood politics: Race, culture, and identity in the Cherokee Nation of Oklahoma.* Berkeley, CA: University of California Press.

[9] O'Donohue, J. (2008) *Anam ćara.* Tribute ed. Transworld Ireland.

## Part VII
### *Sacred Leadership*

[1] Talkpoint (2018) 'Sacred Leadership' Talkpoint. Available from: http://www.talkpoint.com.au/sacredleadership/?mc_cid=412546f886&mc_eid=76677f5532.

[2] Goreng Goreng, T. (2018) Tjukurpa Pulka: The road to eldership: How Aboriginal culture creates sacred and visionary leaders. PhD thesis, Australian National University.

[3] Stanford (2010) 'Kegan's theory of the evolution of consciousness' Tomorrow's Professor Postings. Available from: https://tomprof.stanford.edu/posting/1110#targetText=Kegan%20(Robert)%20introduced%20his%20theory,his%20book%2C%20The%20Evolving%20Self.&targetText=Growth%20involves%20movement%20through%20five,forms%20of%20mind%20in%202000 [Accessed 30 October 2019].

# Goddess Glossary

**Akna:** (Inuit) goddess of childbirth, fertility, motherhood
**Aletheia:** (Greek) goddess of truth, sincerity
**Amaterasu:** (Japanese) celestial sun goddess
**Anahita:** (Persian) goddess of water, fertility, protector of women
**Andraste:** (Celtic) goddess of war, victory
**Aphrodite:** (Greek) goddess of love, beauty, sensuality
**Artemis:** (Greek) goddess of hunting, wild animals, forests, young women, childbirth, fertility, chastity
**Astraea:** (Greek) goddess of justice, innocence, purity, precision
**Athena:** (Greek) goddess of wisdom, war, crafts
**Baba Yaga:** (Slavic) goddess of birth, death, underworld
**Bastet:** (Egyptian) goddess of the home, domesticity, women's secrets
**Benzaiten:** (Japanese) goddess of literature, music, wealth, femininity
**Brighde:** (Celtic) goddess of fire, power, strength
**Ceres:** (Roman) goddess of agriculture
**Cerridwen:** (Celtic) goddess of transformation, rebirth
**Clementia:** (Roman) goddess of forgiveness, mercy, redemption
**Coventina:** (Celtic) goddess of wells, springs, abundance, prophecy
**Cybele:** (Anatolian) mother of the gods, nature
**Danu:** (Celtic) goddess of earth, fertility, wisdom, wind, Celtic people
**Demeter:** (Greek) goddess of the harvest, grain, fertility
**Diana:** (Roman) goddess of the hunt, moon, nature
**Dike:** (Greek) goddess of justice, morality
**Elpis:** (Greek) goddess of hope, fame, rumour
**Eostre:** (Germanic) goddess of Spring
**Felicitas:** (Roman) goddess of peace, prosperity
**Fides:** (Roman) goddess of trust, faith
**Gaia:** (Greek) primal Mother Earth goddess
**Hathor:** (Egyptian) goddess of love, joy, fertility, women
**Hecate:** (Greek) goddess of magic, witchcraft, the night, the moon

**Hella:** (Norse) goddess of the dead
**Inanna:** (Mesopotamian) goddess of love, beauty, sex, desire, fertility
**Isis:** (Egyptian) goddess of magic, fertility, motherhood, death, healing, rebirth
**Ix Chel:** (Maya) goddess of fertility, midwifery, medicine, weaving
**Kali:** (Hindu) goddess of liberation, protection, destruction, transformation
**Kuan Yin:** (Chinese) goddess of mercy, compassion
**Lilith:** (Sumerian) goddess of power, sensuality, liberation
**Maat:** (Egyptian) goddess of truth, justice, balance, morality
**Mami Wata:** (African) goddess of waters, divination, luck, money
**Mazu:** (Chinese) goddess and patroness of the sea
**Metis:** (Greek) goddess of good counsel, planning, cunning, wisdom
**Mo'o:** (Polynesian) goddess of water spirits, mermaids
**Morrigan:** (Celtic) goddess of birth, battle, death
**Mother Mary:** (Christian) goddess of mothers, virgins, sacrifice, service
**Nephthys:** (Egyptian) goddess of the dead, rivers, night, childbirth, mothers
**Ostara:** (Germanic) goddess of Spring, dawn
**Pachamama:** (Andean) goddess of fertility, planting, harvesting, mother earth
**Papahānaumoku:** (Hawaiian) mother earth
**Papatūānuku:** (Maori) mother earth
**Persephone:** (Greek) goddess of Spring
**Rhea:** (Greek) goddess of female fertility, motherhood, generation
**Rhiannon:** (Celtic) goddess of faeries, communication, rest, fertility, horses
**Sága:** (Norse) goddess of songs, poetry, runes, history
**Saraswati:** (Hindu) goddess of knowledge, music, art, wisdom, learning
**Sekhmet:** (Egyptian) goddess of the sun, war, destruction, plagues, healing
**Sige:** (Gnostic) goddess of silence
**Sophia:** (Greek) goddess of wisdom
**Tara:** (Buddhist) goddess of compassion, protection
**Veritas:** (Roman) goddess of truth
**Vesta:** (Roman) goddess of the hearth, home, family
**Zywie:** (Slavic) goddess of life, health, healing

# Bibliography

Academy of Sacred Geometry (2019) *The Eleusinian Mysteries.* Available from: http://www.academysacredgeometry.com/articles/eleusinian-mysteries [Accessed 24 October 2019].

Ambros, B. (2015) *Women in Japanese religions.* New York: New York University Press.

Baring, A. and Cashford, J. (1991) *The myth of the Goddess: Evolution of an image.* London: Viking Arkana.

Bernard, C. (2015) *Queen Himiko: Badass women in Japanese history.* Available from: https://www.tofugu.com/japan/queen-himiko/

Blundell, S. and Williamson, M. (1947-1998) *The sacred and the feminine in ancient Greece.* London: Routledge.

Broderick, M. (2001) *Wild Irish women: Extraordinary lives from history.* Dublin: O'Brien Press.

Brown, D. H. (2003) *Santería enthroned: Art, ritual, and innovation in an Afro-Cuban religion.* Chicago: University of Chicago Press.

Bruhns, K. O. and Stothert, K. (1999) *Women in ancient America.* 2nd ed. Oklahoma: University of Oklahoma Press.

Cartwright, M. (2017) 'Queen Himiko' *Ancient history encyclopedia.* Available from: https://www.ancient.eu/Queen_Himiko/

Cole, S. G. (2004) *Landscapes, gender, and ritual space: The ancient Greek experience.* Berkeley, CA: University of California Press.

Connelly, J. B. (2007) *Portrait of a priestess: Women and ritual in ancient Greece.* Princeton, NJ: Princeton University Press.

Cosmopoulos, M. B. (2015) *Bronze Age Eleusis and the origins of the Eleusinian Mysteries.* New York: Cambridge University Press.

Dashu, M. (2000) 'Knocking down straw dolls: A critique of Cynthia Eller's "The myth of matriarchal prehistory: Why an invented past won't give women a future" ' *Suppressedhistories.net.* Available from: http://www.suppressedhistories.net/articles/StrawDolls.pdf [Accessed 24 October 2019].

DiLuzio, M. J. (2016) *A place at the altar: Priestesses in republican Rome.* Princeton, NJ: Princeton University Press.

DuBois, T. A. (1999) *Nordic religions in the Viking Age.* Philadelphia, PA: University of Pennsylvania Press.

Eisler, R. (1989) 'Reclaiming Our Goddess Heritage', in Nicholson, S. J. (ed.) *The Goddess re-awakening: The feminine principle today.* 1st ed. Wheaton, IL: Theosophical Publishing House, pp. 27-39.

Flower, M. A. (2008) *The seer in ancient Greece.* Berkeley, CA: University of California Press.

Graham, L. D. (2019) 'King's daughter, God's wife: The princess as high priestess in Mesopotamia (Ur, ca. 2300-1100 BCE) and Egypt (Thebes, ca. 1550-525 BCE)' *Scribd.* Available from: https://www.scribd.com/document/360126627/King-s-Daughter-God-s-Wife-The-Princess-as-High-Priestess-in-Mesopotamia-Ur-ca-2300-1100-BCE-and-Egypt-Thebes-ca-1550-525-BCE [Accessed 24 October 2019].

Guiley, R. E. (2001) *The encyclopedia of saints.* New York: Facts on File, Inc.

Haag, M. (2016) *The quest for Mary Magdalene: History & legend.* London: Profile Books.

Haughton, B. (2011) 'The Pythia – Priestess of ancient Delphi' *Ancient History Encyclopedia.* Available from: https://www.ancient.eu/article/205

History.com Editors (2018) 'Hatshepsut' *History.* Available from: https://www.history.com/topics/ancient-history/hatshepsut

Huffman, J. (1997) 'Unearthing the Moche: The bioarchaeology of San Jose de Moro, Peru' *Totem: The University of Western Ontario Journal of Anthropology* 3, no. 1, article 5. Available at: http://ir.lib.uwo.ca/totem/vol3/iss1/5

Jones, G. H. (2013) Pythia'' *Ancient History Encyclopedia.* Available from: https://www.ancient.eu/Pythia/

Keller, M. L. (2009) 'Ritual path of initiation into the Eleusinian Mysteries' *Rosicrucian Digest,* no. 2, pp. 28-42.

Keller, R. S., Ruether, R. R. and Cantlon, M. (2006) *The encyclopedia of women and religion in North America.* Bloomington, IN: Indiana University Press.

Kissane, N. (2017) *Saint Brigid of Kildare: Life, legend and cult.* Dublin: Four Courts Press.

Koch, J. T. (2006) *Celtic culture: A historical encyclopedia.* Santa Barbara, CA: ABC-CLIO.

Lardinois, A. P. M. H. and McClure, L. (1959-2001) *Making silence speak: Women's voices in Greek literature and society.* Princeton, NJ: Princeton University Press.

Lewis, S. (2002) *The Athenian woman: An iconographic handbook.* London and New York: Routledge.

Lindner, M. M. (2015) *Portraits of the Vestal Virgins, priestesses of ancient Rome.* Ann Arbor, MI: University of Michigan Press.

MacLeod, S. P. (2014) *Divine feminine in ancient Europe: Goddesses, sacred women and the origins of Western culture.* Jefferson, NC: McFarland & Co.

Mark, J. J. (2009) ''Vestal Virgin' *Ancient History Encyclopedia.* Available from: https://www.ancient.eu/Vestal_Virgin/

Mark, J. J. (2014) 'Enheduanna' *Ancient History Encyclopedia.* Available from: https://www.ancient.eu/Enheduanna/

Mark, J. J. (2016) 'Hatshepsut' *Ancient History Encyclopedia.* Available from: https://www.ancient.eu/hatshepsut/

Mark, J. J. (2017) 'God's Wife of Amun' *Ancient History Encyclopedia.* Available from: https://www.ancient.eu/God's_Wife_of_Amun/

McCoy, E. (2015) *Celtic women's spirituality: Accessing the cauldron of life.* Woodbury, MN: Llewellyn Publications.

Noble, V. (2003) *The double Goddess: Women sharing power.* Rochester, VT: Bear & Co.

Norse Mythology for Smart People (2019) 'Shamanism' *Norse mythology for smart people.* Available from: https://norse-mythology.org/concepts/shamanism/ [Accessed 24 October 2019].

Norse Mythology for Smart People (n.d.) 'Seidr' *Norse mythology for smart people.* Available from: https://norse-mythology.org/concepts/seidr/ [Accessed 24 October 2019].

Ransome, H. M. (2004) *The sacred bee in ancient times and folklore.* Mineola, NY: Dover.

Rigoglioso, M. (2010) *Virgin mother goddesses of antiquity.* New York: Palgrave Macmillan.

Sanchez-Parodi, J. (2012) 'The Eleusinian Mysteries and the bee' *Ancient History Encyclopedia.* Available from: https://www.ancient.eu/article/341/

Schaus, M. (2016) *Women and gender in medieval Europe: An encyclopedia.* Abingdon, Oxon.: Routledge.

Smith, B. G. (1940-2008) *The Oxford encyclopedia of women in world history.* Oxford: Oxford University Press.

Staples, A. (1998) *From good goddess to vestal virgins: Sex and category in Roman religion.* London: Routledge.

Tyldesley, J. (2018) 'Hatshepsut: Biography, reign, & facts' *Encyclopædia Britannica.* Available from: https://www.britannica.com/biography/Hatshepsut

Weber, C. (2015) *Brigid: History, mystery, and magick of the Celtic goddess.* Newburyport, MA: Weiser Books.

Werner, M. S. (2001) *Concise encyclopedia of Mexico.* Chicago, IL: Fitzroy Dearborn.

Wikipedia (2019) *Aconia Fabia Paulina,* 27 October 2019. Available from: https://en.wikipedia.org/wiki/Aconia_Fabia_Paulina

Willoughby, H. R. (1929) *Pagan regeneration: Chapter II: The greater mysteries at Eleusis.* Available from: https://www.sacred-texts.com/cla/pr/pro4.htm [Accessed 24 October 2019].

Winters, R. (2016) 'Eighth priestess and precious grave goods unearthed in famous San Jose de Moro tomb' *Ancient Origins.* Available from: https://www.ancient-origins.net/news-history-archaeology/eighth-priestess-and-precious-grave-goods-unearthed-famous-san-jose-de-moro-020961?nopaging=1 [Accessed 24 October 2019].

Winters, R. (2016) 'Performance and power: Moche priestesses uncovered' *Ancient Origins.* Available from: https://www.ancient-origins.net/history-famous-people/performance-and-power-moche-priestesses-uncovered-006403 writer873 (2012) 'Vestal virgins of Rome: Privileged keepers of Rome's home fires' *Ancient history encyclopedia*. Available from: https://www.ancient.eu/article/146/

Zissos, A. (2016) *A companion to the Flavian age of imperial Rome*. Chichester, UK; Malden, MA: John Wiley & Sons.

# Index

ableism 262
Aconia Fabia Paulina (Roman aristocrat) 88
Acropolis 50, 79
African liberation movements 95
Afro-Cuban religion 65
Ahmose (Egyptian queen) 75
Akna (Inuit goddess) 8, 288
Alba, Scotland 83
Aletheia (Greek goddess) 144, 288
Algeria 91
al-Kahina, Dahia 160 see Dahia al-Kahina
altar as personal sacred place 164-5
Amaterasu (Japanese goddess) 86, 288
Amun, God's Wife of 43-4, 75-6
Anahita (Persian goddess) 121, 288
Anatolia 40
ancestry 161-3
Andraste (Celtic goddess) 80-82, 288
Aphrodite (Greek goddess) 49, 138-9, 149, 288
Apollo, Temple of 51
apology 141-2
appearance, concern with one's 107
appropriation, cultural 163
art 232-3
Artemis (Greek goddess) 47-9, 146, 154, 288
Astraea (Greek goddess) 118, 288
astrology 22, 180
Athena (Greek goddess) 121, 288
Athena Polias 50, 79
Athens 50, 79
Authentic Freedom Academy 37
Autumn Equinox 174-5, 178-9

Avalon *xxi*, 215

Baba Yaga (Slavic goddess) 152, 288
Babylonians 10, 73, 180
Baghaï, Algeria 91
Bastet (Egyptian goddess) 116, 288
bees 19, 49
Belgrade 77
Bel-Shalti-Nannar see Ennigaldi-Nanna
Beltane 174-5, 177
Benzaiten (Japanese goddess) 121, 288
Berbers 91
betrayal by other women 209
birth family 161-2
Blood Mysteries 187-8, 190
Boudicca (Celtic queen) 80-1, 160
breathing practices 213-14
Bridget, Saint see Brigid, Saint
Brighde (Celtic goddess) 89, 288
Brigid, Saint 89-90, 176
Brigid's Grove 37
Bructeri tribe 82
burn-out 145-6
bypassing, spiritual 126-8, 200, 262

calendars 59, 180 see also seasons
capitalism 107, 149, 258-9, 266-7
Castalian Spring 51
Çatal Hüyük 12, 40
Catholicism 29, 65, 92
Celtic
    festivals 174-5
    lineage 37, 162
    priestesses 12, 55-6
    religion 89, 180

295

society, ancient 55-6
spiritual practices 215
Central America 59-60, 65
Ceres (Roman goddess) 88, 288
Cerridwen (Celtic goddess) 109, 124-5, 288
change, fear of and need for 197-9
Cherokee people 188
childbirth 189-90
Christianity *see also* Catholicism
  among Vikings 58
  in Britain 56
  and Mayan culture 60
  and menstruation 188-9
  and pagan religion 89
  resistance to 94
  rise and spread of 44, 46
Chrysis (Greek priestess) 79
cisgender people *xxv*, 259
Clementia (Roman goddess) 142, 288
Collings, Jane Hardwicke 133
commercialisation 149-50 *see also* capitalism
conservation, environmental 47-8
cooking, spiritual meaning of 19
Coventina (Celtic goddess) 146, 288
Cuba 65, 96-7
Cú Chulainn (epic hero) 83
cultural appropriation 163
cultural background 161-3
  of reader *xxvi-xxvii*
Cybele (Anatolian goddess) 49, 88, 288
cycle of life 200-2

Dahia al-Kahina (Moorish prophetess) 91, 160
dance 66, 92, 207, 232-3
Danu (Celtic goddess) 148, 288
dark, fear of 125
Dark Goddess 139-40, 179
Delphi 51

Demeter (Greek goddess) 45-6, 49, 88, 288
Diana (Roman goddess) 49, 146, 154, 288
Dike (Greek goddess) 118, 288
divination 52, 82, 105, 234-5
dream interpretation 52
Druidism 55-6, 89

ego 110-13
Egypt, ancient 12, 41, 43-4
Egyptians 10, 180
Einstein, Albert (scientist) 264
Eleusinian Mysteries 45-6, 79, 88
Eleusis (in Ancient Greece) 45, 88
Elpis (Greek goddess) 116, 288
Enheduanna 71-2
Ennigaldi-Nanna 73-4
environmental conservation 47-8
Eostre (Germanic goddess) 288
Ephesus 47
Ereshkigal (Mesopotamian goddess) 38, 109
European colonisation 94

family of birth 160-2
fat shaming 259
Felicitas (Roman goddess) 116, 288
Fidelm (Irish priestess) 83
Fides (Roman goddess) 144, 288
Freyja (Norse goddess) 58, 138-9

Gaia (Greek goddess) 8, 150, 288
Geisler, Tanya 23
Germany 82
Glenn (author's husband) 28, 162, 186
goddesses 10-13, 103-6, 289-90
gods 10, 14
God's Wife of Amun 43-4, 75-6
Gómez Pastrana, Fermina (Cuban santera) 96-7

Gonzalez, Ma Monserrate (priestess) 96
Goreng Goreng, Dr Tjanara 249–50
gospels, Christian 84
Great Goddess 8
Great Mother 8–9, 15, 135, 150, 171–3
Great Ziggurat of Ur 73
Greeks, ancient 10, 12, 50, 180
Grimm, Jacob (mythologist) 174

Hades (king of the underworld) 88
Haiti 63, 65
Hathor (Egyptian goddess) 41, 288
Hatshepsut (ruler of Egypt) 44, 75–6
healing/healthcare, as role of priestess xxvi, 8, 12, 41, 66, 145, 236–7
Hebrew calendar 180
Hecate (Greek goddess) 88, 109, 152, 288
Hella (Norse goddess) 109, 131, 289
hemet-netjer 41–2
Henry, Archbishop of Dublin 89
herbalism 66
heteronormativity 124, 259
Himiko (Yamatai queen) 86–7
honesty 122 *see also* truth-telling
horoscope *see* astrology; divination

Iceni tribe 80
Imbolc 174–7
imperfection 141
imposter complex 23
Inanna (Mesopotamian goddess) 38, 71, 289
industrialisation 200
Isis (Egyptian goddess) 41, 44, 88, 125, 146, 154, 289
Israel, ancient 84
Ix Chel (Mayan goddess) 59, 289

Japan, ancient 86

Jenks, Sarah 20–1
Jesus Christ 84
judgement of self and others 117–18

*kahina* (seer) 90
Kalasha Valley, Pakistan 188
Kali (Hindu goddess) 125, 131, 289
Kassem, Suzy (visionary) 264
Kegan, Professor Robert 250
Kildare County, Ireland 89
Kojouri, Kamand (poet) 264
Kuan Yin (Chinese goddess) 113, 117, 142, 289
Kulin Nations 162

Laveau, Marie 92–3, 160
leadership, meaning of 246–7
Lilith (Sumerian goddess) 152, 289
Litha (Summer Solstice) 174–5, 177–8
lucumí 65
Lughnasadh 174–5, 178
lunar energy *see* moon

Maat (Egyptian goddess) 121, 289
Mabon (Autumn Equinox) 174–5, 178–9
Magdala 84
mambos 63–4
Mami Wata (African goddess) 131, 289
Mary, Mother of Jesus *see* Mother Mary
Mary Magdalene, Saint 84–5
Mayan people 12, 59–60
Mazu (Chinese goddess) 131, 289
Medb (Connacht queen) 83
medical services *see* healing/healthcare
meditation 106, 138, 147, 169
*melissai* 49
menarche 187–8, 204
menopause 188–9, 204–5

menstrual cycle 181–2, 187–96
Mesoamerica 59–60, 65
Mesopotamia 10, 12, 38, 73, 104
Metis (Greek goddess) 128, 289
midwives 12, 59–60
misogyny, internalised 115
Moche 61–2
monotheism 14
moon 178–84, 192
13 Moon Mystery School 37
Mo'o (Polynesian goddess) 116, 289
Morrigan (Celtic goddess) 131, 152, 289
Mother *see* Great Mother
Mother Earth 8, 150, 289–90
Mother Mary (Christian goddess) 113, 289
Mother Nature 8, 150
music 232–3
Mysteries, Blood 187–8, 190
Mysteries, Eleusinian 45–6, 79, 88
mystery schools 36–7, 45

Nabonidus (king of Ur) 73
Nanna (god) 73
nature *see also* wilderness
  disconnection from 267–8
Nefertari (Egyptian queen) 44
Nehanda (oracle) 94
Neo-Paganism 174
Nephthys (Egyptian goddess) 41, 109, 289
Nero (Roman king) 79
New Orleans 92–3
Nicks, Stevie 29
No, Sora Surya 27
nomads 14
Nyakasikana, Nehanda Charwe 94–5

Oba Tero (priestess) 96
Odin (Norse god) 162
O'Donohue, John (philosopher) 216

Olókun (ancestral spirit) 96–7
Onomaris (Celtic priestess) 77–8
Orishas 65–6, 96
Ostara (Germanic goddess) 289
Ostara (Spring Equinox) 174–5, 177

Pachamama (Andean goddess) 8, 150, 289
pagan rituals stamped out 46
Panathenaia, Greater 50
Papahānaumoku (Hawaiian mother earth) 8, 289
Papatūānuku (Maori mother earth) 8, 150, 289
patriarchy *xxiv*, 14, 27, 60, 107, 206, 213
  and internalised misogyny 115
  and menstruation 188–9
  suppression of female power 85–6
people-pleasing 125, 160, 206
perfection, letting go of 114–16
Persephone (Greek goddess) 45, 88, 289
Persian invasion of Egypt 44
Peru 61
Plato (Greek philosopher) 45
privilege 258–63
psychic abilities 228–9
Pythia 51–2

racism 123, 259–60, 262
raiders, nomadic 14
Regla del Ocha 65
responsibility 110–11
Rhea (Greek goddess) 49, 289
Rhiannon (Celtic goddess) 142, 289
rites of passage 204
Roman religion 88
Romans 10, 56, 80, 180
Rome, ancient 12, 53–4

sacred place, personal 164–5

Sága (Norse goddess) 128, 289
Samhain 174-6
*sanga* 38-9
Santería 65-6, 96
Saraswati (Hindu goddess) 121, 289
Sargon (king of Agade) 71
Scandinavia 162
School of Shamanic Womancraft 37, 133, 143
Scotland 215
seasons 174-9, 191-3
Seidr 57-8
Sekhmet (Egyptian goddess) 131, 289
Selçuk (Turkey) 47
Selene (Greek goddess) 181
self-care 145-6
Sena (island) 55
sexuality 262
Shamanic Womancraft, School of 37, 133, 143
shame, menstrual 188-9
Si (Moche goddess) 61
Sige (Gnostic goddess) 148, 289
Singidunum, Serbia 77
sister wounds 209-11
slavery 65, 97
sleep 182
smoke machine 28-9
social media 107, 117, 123, 132, 153
Socrates (Greek philosopher) 45
Sophia (Gnostic goddess) 148
Sophia (Greek goddess) 144, 289
soul friends 215-16
Spanish colonisation 60
spiritual awakening/experience 19-20, 133-4, 139-40
Spring Equinox 174-5, 177
stillness 147-8
Sumer(ians) 12, 38-9, 71, 180
Summer Solstice 174, 177-8

Tara (Buddhist goddess) 113, 118, 142, 289
Teilhard de Chardin, Pierre 264
Theodosius I (Roman emperor) 46, 54
Thutmose I (Egyptian pharaoh) 75
Thutmose III (Egyptian pharaoh) 75-6
transgender people 187, 262
transphobia *xxv*, 118, 265
trusting yourself *xxvii*
truth, nature of *xxv*
truth-telling 119-21

Ur 73

Veleda (Bructeri priestess) 82
Veritas (Roman goddess) 121, 128, 289
Vestal priestesses 53-4
Vesta (Roman goddess) 53, 227, 289
Vikings 57, 162
Vodou 63-4, 92
Völur 57-8

Welwood, John (psychotherapist) 126
Wheel of the Year 174-5, 224
white privilege 123, 259-60
Wicca 174-5
wilderness 133, 143-4
Winter Solstice 174, 176
'woman', definition of *xxv*
Wurundjeri People 162

Yamatai (in ancient Japan) 86-7
Yoruba 65, 96
Yule (Winter Solstice) 174, 176

Ziggurat of Ur 73
Zimbabwe 94
zodiac *see* astrology
Zywie (Slavic goddess) 146, 289

www.ingramcontent.com/pod-product-compliance
Lightning Source LLC
Chambersburg PA
CBHW020315010526
44107CB00054B/1845